A FIRST BOOK OF METAL-WORK

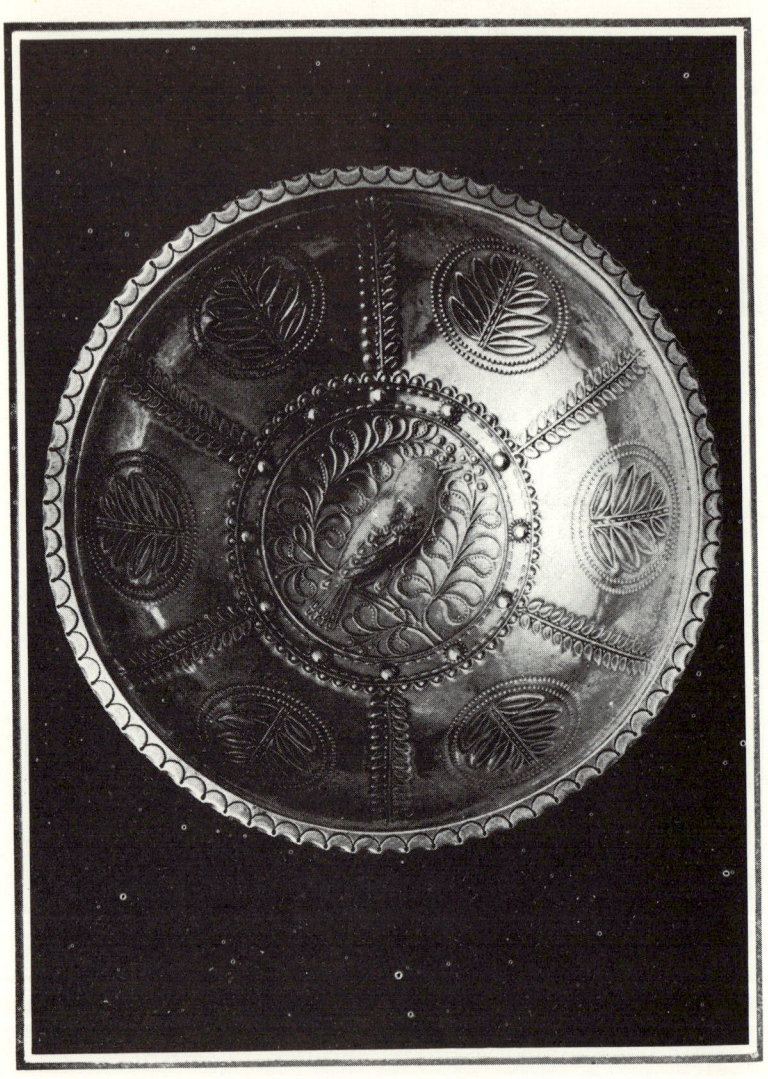

PLATE I.—A Silver Bowl made by the Author.

[*Frontispiece*

A FIRST BOOK OF METAL-WORK

BY
BERNARD CUZNER
Former Head of the Department of Metal-work in Birmingham Central School of Arts and Crafts

FOREWORD BY
ANDREW SMITH C. Eng
Member of the College of Handicrafts
Member of the Royal Society of Teachers

Gresham Books

©Unwin Brothers Limited and Bernard Cuzner, 1979

All rights reserved. No part of
this book may be reproduced in
any form or by any means without
the permission of the publisher.

First published in original form 1931
This revised edition 1979

ISBN 0 905418 54 9

Gresham Books,
Unwin Brothers Limited,
The Gresham Press,
Old Woking, Surrey,
England.

Printed in Great Britain
by Unwin Brothers Limited
The Gresham Press,
Old Woking, Surrey

"And look that thou make them after their pattern, which was shewed thee in the mount."—Exod. xxv. 40.

"But every work of art . . . has one indispensable mark—I mean, that the centre of it is simple, however much the fulfilment may be complicated."—G. K. CHESTERTON.

"Real development is not leaving things behind, as on a road, but drawing life from them, as from a root."—G. K. CHESTERTON.

"We are always agonising about design, but design, as Rodin has said, is as nothing compared to workmanship."—W. R. LETHABY.

FOREWORD

It gave me great pleasure to become re-acquainted with a book first used when a student of craftwork nearly forty years ago. And it is a salutory thought that its adherence to true craft principles and a feeling for the material being worked, has meant more to me on this second reading.

The author's comments in his "Introductory" chapter about a second book raises the question, "was this book ever produced?"

Readers will appreciate that the book deals with a period now long past — an ounce of silver, plated on a bowl for 10/- (50p), or a 6 inch diameter disc of silver for £1.2s.6d. (£1.12½p)! But the appeal of real craftsmanship still exists and Bernard Cuzner's instructions show how such skills can be developed with simple and inexpensive equipment.

A great deal is said in the text about hard and soft solders and their fluxes, often a problem, as I well remember. The availability now commercially of a wide range of these materials and the use of liquified gas appliances for heating, makes such operations more likely to be successful in the hands of the amateur.

All dimensions are in inches and there is little point in altering these throughout the book. The reader need only remember that approximately 25 millimetres equals 1 inch. Similarly 0.040 inch is nearly 1 millimetre, hence the wire and metal gauges on page 12 may be converted with sufficient accuracy by using this figure. For example No. 19 wire gauge will approximate to 1 millimetre, while No. 25 ditto will be 0.5mm.

Finally, in an industrial world of preciseness, how delightful it is to read instructions that say, "a bit as large as a hazel-nut in a pint of water", but how sad the author would be to see our present day lamp-posts!

ANDREW SMITH, C. Eng
Member of the College of Handicrafts,
Member of the Royal Society of Teachers.

INTRODUCTORY

AMONGST the many excellent textbooks on metal-work there would seem to be room for one dealing with absolute first principles.

The following is an attempt at such a book, based upon the writer's experience of more than twenty years of teaching, in the Schools of Art in Birmingham, of all sorts and conditions of students, from young boys of eleven, still attending elementary schools, to competent, highly trained art students, and professional workers in the metal industries.

In the course of his experience the writer has found that, once a student has grasped firmly the basic principles of the craft, the attainment of proficiency is chiefly a matter of steady work.

The system advocated and the practical instructions given are identical with those the writer uses in his own classes. The illustrations are drawn from sketches of the type he is making constantly in the course of teaching.

The first chapter deals with the material, its nature and properties. Even a brief study of fine metal-work of all ages and of all countries will show us how all-important it is that the craftsman should understand his material and, as it were, sympathise with it.

Chapter II describes the tools. Here we may note that, though every craftsman wishes for a complete equipment, it is but rarely that he can attain his desire. Fortunately for the metal-worker, many of his tools are extremely simple. Substitutes can often be improvised from things found on a scrap-heap; these, apart from the fact that they may look somewhat clumsy, are just as good as expensive bought tools; beyond this the metal-worker is often able himself to make many of his own tools and appliances.

Chapter III is divided into sections dealing with various processes and the principles involved in their use. These should be read in conjunction with the instructions for making the twelve articles described in the lessons.

Chapter IV begins with a series of six preliminary lessons. These may be omitted by the student who has some experience of metal-work. For the absolute beginner they are most valuable.

The too common bane of school metal-work is that elaborate pieces are attempted before the student has learned the use of the essential tools. Each tool, as it works, gives what the writer chooses to call an idiom of the craft. Each tool yields its own particular quality of surface or form. From the first the student should be taught how valuable these are, and how they should be used.

Of all crafts, metal-work demands the highest standard of accuracy. If, from the very beginning, the student is accustomed to work as exactly as he can, the extreme precision needed in the later stages will come naturally, and with comparatively little effort. The six preliminary lessons have been devised with the acquisition of clean accurate workmanship as their chief aim.

The lessons that follow deal, as will be seen at once, with construction rather than decoration, the exception being the process of saw piercing. Here again the order has been chosen with the object of training the student in essentials. A second and supplementary series of notes on processes and lessons will, if the success of the present book warrants it, be published at an early date.

These will deal with more advanced problems of technique, with the decorative processes, and will include a series of twenty-four objects chosen in the main as being useful, yet capable of being made interesting, and affording scope for the exercise of the student's creative abilities.

This book deals with the methods used by the worker in silver and fine bronze and brass. The choice is deliberate. It has been proved over and over again that these fine metal crafts have a far higher educational value than the more utilitarian branches of sheet metal and smith's work. The former, as usually practised, affords very little scope for the imagination; and the latter, on the scale possible in schools, cannot go very far. Students who are familiar with these, will find the knowledge offered in the present book a most valuable complement, and it will enable them to add a refinement and interest to metal-work, no matter of what kind, or on what scale it may be. Again, the fineness of the technique needed for the work treated of in this book will be of the greatest help in all other branches.

If we enquire into the origins of the engines and machines that have made modern civilisation possible, we shall find that the men who first worked them out were engaged, not on purely utilitarian work, but on work that we, in this present day, would think of as decorative. The truth is, of course, that only men with eyes and hands trained, as the fine metal-workers have to be trained, can reach the essential standard of accuracy without recourse to elaborate mechanical means. The writer claims, confidently, that even for those students whose work is mechanical rather than artistic, the course advocated has extreme value.

Chapter V is intended for the teachers who will use this book, rather than for young students. It consists of a short statement of the æsthetic principles of metal-work as the writer sees them. He hopes that they will be sufficient to stimulate his readers to think things out for themselves, and to build up an æsthetic of their own. The whole question is such a vast one that we can see but one facet of it at one time, and each one of us will see it from a different angle. It is of vital importance that the teacher should be able to give a reason for his beliefs and tastes. To teach successfully, the teacher must be completely convinced in his own mind that what he advocates is right. Too often a student wastes his powers, simply because he has no clear idea of what he is doing or in which direction he is moving.

Lastly, in Chapter VI a series of illustrations of simple metal-work is given, with a short note on each. These will show how, from the simplest works, valuable lessons can be learned.

Metal-workers should never lose a chance of looking out for interesting objects. Even now, in this mechanical age, some wholly right and delightful things survive ; and things of pure utility made solely for efficiency will often teach the craftsman most valuable lessons.

CONTENTS

CHAPTER		PAGE
	FOREWORD	vii
	INTRODUCTORY	ix
I.	THE MATERIAL	1
II.	THE METAL-WORKER'S TOOLS . .	13
III.	SECTION 1. THE HAMMERING OF METALS	27
	SECTION 2. THE HEATING AND FUSION OF METALS	37
	SECTION 3. CUTTING METALS . .	43
	SECTION 4. DRILLING, RIVETING, AND WIRE DRAWING	50
	SECTION 5. POLISHING AND FINISHING .	58
	SECTION 6. PIERCING	64
IV.	INTRODUCTORY	68
	LESSON 1. FILING A CHISEL . .	71
	LESSON 2. CUTTING PLATES . .	75
	LESSON 3. MAKING A "CENTRE" PUNCH	78
	LESSON 4. MAKING A SCRIBER . .	80
	LESSON 5. DRILL MAKING (SPEAR OR DIAMOND POINT)	81

CONTENTS

CHAPTER		PAGE
LESSON 6.	ESCUTCHEON COMPLETED	85
LESSON 7.	A SIMPLE DISH OR TRAY	89
LESSON 8.	RAISING, HAMMERING, AND MOUNTING A BOWL	105
LESSON 9.	A CIGARETTE BOX	122
LESSON 10.	A CIRCULAR BOX WITH A LID	130
LESSON 11.	SERVIETTE RING DECORATED WITH CORDED WIRES	138
LESSON 12.	A TEA-POT STAND (PIERCED)	145
V. SOME PRINCIPLES		153
VI. NOTES ON THE PHOTOGRAPHIC PLATES		160

PLATES

PLATE
I. A SILVER BOWL . . . *Frontispiece*

                                                                             FACING PAGE

II. A HORSE BRASS AND A CLOCK FRET . 64

III. ENGLISH AND FRENCH WATCH COCKS . 128

IV. SUGAR NIPPERS, BOX LID, AND A PIN VICE 129

V. A WOODEN CASTING PATTERN, A BUCKLE, AND SERVIETTE RINGS . . . 144

VI. A TEA CADDY 145

A FIRST BOOK OF METAL-WORK

CHAPTER I

THE MATERIAL

The material and its properties—The two classes of metals—The ferrous metals—The non-ferrous metals, base and precious—Alloys or mixed metals—Alloys of precious metals—Fusible alloys or solders: Hard—Flux for Hard solder—Soft solders and flux.

WHATEVER craft we consider, a little thought will show us the primary importance of understanding and appreciating rightly the peculiar inherent qualities and properties of its materials. The nature of these determines not only the tools that are used, and the methods of working, but to a far greater extent than is commonly recognised, the forms into which the material is wrought.

If we consider the crafts of the worker in wood, in stone, pottery, glass, plaster, leather, we see at once how different are the qualities of form the different materials assume under the different tools. The caligrapher and the weaver will often use the same motive of decoration, but how different are the results.

Let us accept as a principle without hesitation that the finer the work the more does it show appreciation and understanding of its material.

Metals differ from all other substances in combining plasticity with strength, and hardness with elasticity.

They have, moreover, a beauty of surface and lustre peculiarly their own.

Yet with all its differences metal has many likenesses to other substances. We can cut it as we do wood and stone. We can force it into moulds as clay and glass. We can make it liquid and pour it into moulds as we do plaster. We can even make metal into long thin threads (wires) and weave them. Its range is greater than that of any other substance. So is its strength also.

The one fact we must never lose sight of is this—we can make metal change its shape without altering its nature and strength, and without removing any of its substance. Lastly, and this is especially important in the case of precious metals, the scrap and filings, even to the tiniest speck, can be melted and used over again.

THE QUALITIES AND PROPERTIES OF METALS

We may say that there are three qualities of metals which they share with other substances truly, but which the metal-worker must ever keep firmly and clearly in his mind. They are:

Strength.—The metal-worker can therefore work on a scale of thicknesses impossible in other substances.

Durability.—Works in metal, having such endurance, must be of such fineness of form and workmanship that their owners and users will for ever give thanks because they are imperishable.

Beauty.—Metal can be wrought into forms of the utmost fineness and subtlety. Its colour, not only beautiful in itself, but so clearly in harmony with metal forms, that colour and form are but different aspects: its lustre of surface, so peculiarly metallic and so different from all else: the appreciation and understanding of these help and inspire the worker.

THE MATERIAL

It may be noted that metals are the best conductors of heat and electricity.

The properties of metals which concern the actual working are:

Malleability.—Metals can be made to change their shape by force, by hammer blows, or by steady pressure—whichever is the more conveniently applied.

Fusibility.—Metals can be melted by heat until they are completely liquid, and we can pour—cast—them into moulds of any shape we wish.

Ductility.—We can lead or pull—draw—metal into long rods or wires of any section.

THE TWO CLASSES OF METALS

The first metals to be discovered by man were gold, copper, and tin. Copper especially was a substance from which tools and weapons could be fashioned that did not chip and break. It marked an advance that must have seemed final. Yet the interval that separated this discovery from the next, that opened out far wider possibilities, cannot have been, comparatively speaking, very long.

Somewhere the ores of copper and tin were found and smelted together. Some observant metal-worker then found he had a metal not unlike copper, but of such a superiority in hardness and toughness as to enable him to make tools and weapons vastly better than those of the softer copper. The change from copper to bronze may have meant even more than the change from stone to copper; but there were other discoveries to come more important and revolutionary.

THE FERROUS METALS

With the increase of metallurgical skill man became aware of another metal which made still more efficient weapons. In some places men found great masses of it lying on the ground. It may even have been seen to fall from the heavens. This was iron. Not yet, however, was the way open to complete mastery over the other metals.

Somewhere and somehow iron had taken into its substance one of the commonest elements of the earth —carbon. Iron containing a small percentage of carbon has the remarkable property of becoming intensely hard when heated to redness and cooled suddenly by plunging into water.

This metal, to the eye so like, and in reality so unlike, iron, we call steel. Here men found at last something that gave them the power to do whatever they willed with other metals; something from which they could make tools that would last indefinitely.

For us in this book these " ferrous " metals, iron and steel, are important as being the materials of which our tools are made. Actually, iron will not concern us much excepting that many of our tools and appliances will be cast-iron.

The following facts should be noted :

Cast-iron—the form in which iron is smelted out from the ore. It may contain as much as 3 to 4 per cent. of carbon. This can be melted without difficulty in a furnace—cupola—with a blast. It can then be poured into moulds, usually of sand. In this way heavy things, such as the bases of machinery, are made. Cast-iron is inclined to be brittle in thin pieces.

Malleable cast-iron.—Iron castings of certain quality can have the brittleness taken out of them by a lengthy process of heating. The heads and stakes we shall use will often be made of " malleable cast-iron."

Mild steel.—This contains a very small amount of carbon. It is superior to iron for many purposes, being not only stronger but of finer grain.

THE MATERIAL

Cast steel.—Steel containing ·9 per cent. or more of carbon. This was, before the science of metallurgy had developed, made by heating bars of pure iron in a box packed with animal charcoal. The iron absorbed a small amount of carbon, and in doing so became blistered. For certain purposes this " blister " steel was forged into bars for the cutler and smith to work up. Some time in the eighteenth century it was found that " blister " steel could be melted in a crucible and cast into bars before being hammered or rolled out. The rods and wires which we shall use for tool-making will be cast steel.

The ferrous metals having much higher melting-points, we can use iron and steel tools safely in many of the heating processes to which the other metals are subjected.

THE NON-FERROUS METALS

Taking these in the order of their importance in the course of work set forth in this book first come :

Copper.—This is valuable, not only for its colour, but for its extreme malleability and toughness. Its one failing is softness.

Tin.—Useful ; its melting-point is low, and it is not acted upon by vegetable acids. We can easily coat the interiors of vessels with it, and thus fit them for use as kitchen or table wares. Tin is most familiar to us in the form of " tin plate," of which the cans and boxes containing our food, our luxuries, and countless other things are packed or carried.

Tin plate is simply thin iron plate which has been cleaned by immersion in acid and then dipped in a bath of molten tin until a film of the white metal adheres to it.

Zinc.—Of little use alone excepting for very special purposes.

Lead.—Also only useful for special purposes, mainly on large-scale work. To us it is indispensable for certain appliances.

Aluminium.—Of occasional use only.

Nickel.—Very rarely used pure.

Then in a class by themselves come the three precious metals :

Gold.—The most malleable and ductile of metals, and perhaps the most beautiful. This present book will not deal directly with it.

Platinum.—The heaviest and most infusible of metals. Completely indestructible and untarnishable. On this account used for setting diamonds. Outside the scope of this book.

Silver.—Has of late years become so plentiful as to rank as semi-precious only. Every metal-worker must use it in some form. Many of the exercises given herein may be worked in this delightful metal by the identical methods given.

These three metals do not absorb oxygen from the air when heated to any extent ; so that the action of fire causes no loss of substance or weight. This gained for them the old name of " noble " metals. Acids have less effect upon them than on other metals.

ALLOYS OR MIXED METALS

Few metals are of more than very limited use when pure. Alloys or mixtures are more serviceable and more easily worked. The range of colour is greatly extended. Most important of all, the mixing of metals allows us to control the melting-point of the alloy.

Alloys in Common Use

Brass, a mixture of copper and zinc, is the most important. Its colour is fine, and it has almost all the good working properties combined in itself. It is as useful for casting as it is for wrought work. The proportions of the metals in brass vary very much. Normal standards may be taken as 65 to 75 per cent. copper. Alloys with a low copper content may be worked hot.

Gilding metal.—A name given to a brass so rich in copper as to be, when untarnished, almost exactly the colour of gold. For wrought work, superior in working properties to yellow brass. An ordinary gilding metal will probably contain 80 to 90 per cent. of copper.

Bronze.—An alloy of copper and tin. A beautiful metal, but not easy to use for wrought work. For cast work is unsurpassed. By varying the proportion of copper and tin alloys of very different colours can be obtained. These range from the dark-red brown of bronze to the intense white of speculum metal. The degrees of hardness and brittleness also vary enormously. 85 per cent. copper and 15 per cent. tin is a usual mixture.

Nickel, or German-silver.—A white alloy of copper, zinc, and a small amount, 10 per cent. or so, of nickel. A useful rather than a beautiful metal. Excellent for work intended to be electro-plated with silver. Varying proportions of its constituents produce very different working properties. It can be made soft and easily workable, or of extreme hardness and strength.

Pewter.—An alloy of tin, copper, and antimony. Sometimes a little lead is added. It can be wrought, but the fine old pewter ware so highly valued by collectors was first cast in brass moulds, then hammered to make it hard, and finally finished either on the lathe or with scraper and burnisher. It is, of course, easily melted, though it can be soldered.

Britannia-metal.—Similar to pewter. Generally used for making cheap electro-plate.

The commonly used alloys of the precious metals are :

22, 18, 15, 9 *carat gold.*—These are mixtures of gold and copper. Sometimes silver is used, alone or in combination with copper,[1] according to the colour or hardness desired. The numbers refer to the parts of pure gold contained in the 24 " carats " into which the weight of any piece of gold is assumed to be divided—thus, 18 carat has 18 parts of gold and 6 parts of copper.

Standard or sterling silver.—A mixture of 925 parts silver and 75 parts copper. Superior in colour, durability, and working qualities to pure—fine—silver. (Fine silver has a very small range of usefulness.) One of the most delightful of metals to work. It has almost every conceivable good quality. This ·925 alloy is the legal standard, and is stamped with a lion when hall-marked.

Britannia silver.—958·3 parts pure silver in the 1,000, the legal standard in England from 1697 till 1720. It is still used occasionally. Instead of a lion it bears a figure of Britannia.

FUSIBLE ALLOYS OR SOLDERS

One of the most important discoveries about metals was that ores from one place yielded a metal that melted more easily than others. What then more natural than the idea of joining pieces of metal together by melting some of this easily fusible metal between the pieces to be joined ? Sooner or later men could not fail to notice that this variation could be got by mixing metals. With this discovery of soldering an advance of the greatest importance was made.

---

[1] White gold is made by using nickel as well as copper and silver. It is very hard and difficult to work, but useful because it does not tarnish.

THE MATERIAL

THE TWO CLASSES OF SOLDERS

If we look at the table of metals at the end of the chapter, we shall see that while many metals will melt at or above a red heat over 600° or 700° Centigrade, others melt well below. Solders are therefore divided into two classes—*hard*, melting at the higher points, and *soft*, melting at the lower. The latter always contains lead and tin.

HARD SOLDERS.—These, even for the worker in ordinary—" base "—metals, are divided into two classes—brass solders and silver solders.

Brass solder is normally, though there are many variations, half (50 per cent.) copper and half (50 per cent.) zinc. It may be had in sheet or more often in powder or " grain "—the harder solders are yellow, the easier ones are black—and in wire, about 20 S.W.G. thick. Brass solder is therefore a low-grade brass. With it we can solder, or as is more usual to say, " braze " brass of a higher grade, say 68 per cent. copper and 32 per cent. zinc, though this needs much care and experience to do satisfactorily. Cast brass of good quality—" fine "—is more easily brazed than rolled sheet. Gilding metal and copper will be found much easier. There is so much less risk of melting. For these a brass with a higher proportion of copper can be used as a solder.

Silver solder.—This is almost always a mixture of silver, copper, and zinc. Three grades are in common use : *Hardest*, containing silver, 82 per cent., copper, 14 per cent., zinc, 4 per cent. ; *hard*, containing silver, 78 per cent., copper, 15 per cent., zinc, 7 per cent. ; *easy*, containing silver, 67 per cent., copper, 24 per cent., zinc, 9 per cent. All these can be used on work in standard silver.

A system of marking solder should be devised and

used continuously. To attempt to use a piece of the hardest solder where the easy grade is needed is to court disaster. We should be able to recognise even tiny bits of solder at a glance.

The following is a suggestion : For *hardest*, a series of blunt chisel marks, longitudinal. For *hard*, a series of centre-punch marks. For *easy*, scratches in criss-cross fashion.

If there is no intention of working in precious metal, other metals can be soldered with a solder containing silver, 40 per cent., copper, 35 per cent., zinc, 25 per cent., but this is not suitable for silver.

These silver solders are generally used in strips cut from thin sheet, 8 metal gauge, or 25 S.W. gauge, thick for large work, and 4 metal gauge., or 30 S.W. gauge, for small work. The use of silver solders containing tin is not advised. They tend to eat into the metal.[1]

All these solders need a flux, or solvent, for the oxides that form when the metal is raised to a red heat. The almost universally used flux for hard solder is borax. It can be used in powder, dry ; or it can be mixed with water into a cream. This is the most generally useful. For fine small work crystal borax, or a prepared compressed kind, is rubbed, with water, on a slate until a cream is formed. Borax and water are always applied with a camel-hair brush, often called a " borax pencil."

SOFT SOLDERS.—Those in common use are :

Plumber's solder.—Tin, 50 per cent., lead, 50 per cent. This is suitable for rough work only.

Tinman's solder.—Tin, $66\frac{2}{3}$ per cent., lead, $33\frac{1}{3}$ per cent. This is excellent for nearly every purpose.

Pewter solder.—Tin, 62 per cent., lead, 31 per cent., bismuth, 7 per cent. This melts at very low

---

[1] It should be noted that these formulæ are varied very considerably by different refiners and bullion dealers.

THE MATERIAL

temperatures, and may therefore be used to solder pewter.

For soft solders there are three classes of fluxes:

The acid, *chloride of zinc*, often called "*killed spirit.*" This is hydrochloric acid into which pieces of zinc have been dropped until all hydrogen has been driven off and ebullition ceases. This is perhaps the easiest to use. Care should be taken to wash all traces away when the work is done. Proprietary preparations of a similar nature are also to be had.

The resinous.—Especially useful for tinned iron plate, it is simply powdered resin.

The greasy.—For soldering lead plumbers often use tallow. It is not suitable for other metals.

For pewter the best flux is resin dissolved in a cheap olive-oil. Here again proprietary preparations, such as "Fluxite," are to be had, and are excellent for some work.

TABLE OF PROPERTIES OF METALS
All pure metals are elements

Metal.	Specific Gravity.	Tenacity in lb. per square inch.	Melting-point (Centigrade). Degrees.
Silver (pure)	10·47	41,000	958
Silver (standard)	10·312		890
Gold (pure)	19·35	20,400	1,063
Copper	8·85	33,000	1,083
Brass	8·5	40,000	960
Iron (cast)	7·18	19,000	1,130
Iron (wrought)	7·7	60,000	1,600
Steel	7·82	120,000	1,450
Lead	11·35	1,824	326
Tin	7·3	5,000	232
Platinum	21·4	25,000	1,755
Zinc	7·1	22,400	420
Nickel	8·9	67,200	1,452
Aluminium	2·7	12,320	657

NOTES.—*Specific gravity* is the weight of any substance compared with the weight of an equal bulk of water.

Centigrade is the scale of temperature where freezing-point of water = 0, and boiling-point = 100.

IMPERIAL STANDARD WIRE GAUGE

No. 1 = ·300 of 1 in.
,, 2 = ·276 ,, ,,
,, 3 = ·252 ,, ,,
,, 4 = ·232 ,, ,,
,, 5 = ·212 ,, ,,
,, 6 = ·192 ,, ,,
,, 7 = ·176 ,, ,,
,, 8 = ·160 ,, ,,
,, 9 = ·144 ,, ,,
,, 10 = ·128 ,, ,,
,, 11 = ·116 ,, ,,
,, 12 = ·104 ,, ,,
,, 13 = ·092 ,, ,,
,, 14 = ·080 ,, ,,
,, 15 = ·072 ,, ,,
,, 16 = ·064 ,, ,,
,, 17 = ·056 ,, ,,
,, 18 = ·048 ,, ,,

No. 19 = ·040 of 1 in.
,, 20 = ·036 ,, ,,
,, 21 = ·032 ,, ,,
,, 22 = ·028 ,, ,,
,, 23 = ·024 ,, ,,
,, 24 = ·022 ,, ,,
,, 25 = ·020 ,, ,,
,, 26 = ·018 ,, ,,
,, 27 = ·0164 ,, ,,
,, 28 = ·0148 ,, ,,
,, 29 = ·0136 ,, ,,
,, 30 = ·0124 ,, ,,
,, 31 = ·0116 ,, ,,
,, 32 = ·0108 ,, ,,
,, 33 = ·0100 ,, ,,
,, 34 = ·0092 ,, ,,
,, 35 = ·0084 ,, ,,

THE METAL GAUGE

		1 sq. in. of Sheet Silver weighs in oz. Troy.			1 sq. in. of Sheet Silver weighs in oz. Troy.
No. 1 = ·0085 of 1 in.	—	No. 13 = ·038 of 1 in.	·220
,, 2 = ·0095 ,, ,,	—	,, 14 = ·043 ,, ,,	·246
,, 3 = ·0105 ,, ,,	—	,, 15 = ·048 ,, ,,	·268
,, 4 = ·012 ,, ,,	·070	,, 16 = ·051 ,, ,,	·286
,, 5 = ·014 ,, ,,	·081	,, 17 = ·055 ,, ,,	·307
,, 6 = ·016 ,, ,,	·093	,, 18 = ·059 ,, ,,	·330
,, 7 = ·019 ,, ,,	·110	,, 19 = ·062 ,, ,,	·342
,, 8 = ·0215 ,, ,,	·126	,, 20 = ·065 ,, ,,	·362
,, 9 = ·024 ,, ,,	·143	,, 21 = ·069 ,, ,,	—
,, 10 = ·028 ,, ,,	·163	,, 22 = ·073 ,, ,,	—
,, 11 = ·032 ,, ,,	·183	,, 23 = ·077 ,, ,,	—
,, 12 = ·035 ,, ,,	·203	,, 24 = ·082 ,, ,,	—

CHAPTER II
THE METAL-WORKER'S TOOLS

Workshop and benches—Vices and anvil—Flat die or surface plate—Mandrels or ring stakes—Hammers and mallets—Files—Shears, pliers, corn tongs, tongs, hand vice—Stakes—Drills—Measuring appliances—Saws—Screwing tackle—Soldering appliances—Pitch pot and blocks—Polishing appliances and materials—Sand-bag and steady block—Chemicals.

THE WORKSHOP AND ITS FITTINGS

THE equipment described is large enough to undertake a wide range of work. For the twelve exercises given in this book a much simpler one is ample. At the head of each lesson a list of the tools required is given.

Almost any room will serve as a workshop, provided it is well lighted. If possible the benches should be close to a window. Where this is impossible a top light is best. Other desirable conveniences are a hood to carry off the hot air and fumes from the hearths and from the acids, and a sink with water laid on.

The benches should have beech or elm tops 2 in. thick. The legs should be of 3×3 in. deal. The height to top of bench, 2 ft. 9 in. to 3 ft. 3 in., according to stature of the worker. Benches are best fixed firmly to the wall: where this is impossible, cross bracing must be employed to ensure steadiness.

In the edges, it is convenient to cut slots $1\frac{1}{2}$ in. deep, $2\frac{1}{2}$ in. wide, and $\frac{1}{2}$ in. high, into which jewellers' pegs can be put. For work in precious metals some provision for fixing sliding frames on to which leather pockets, or "skins," can be nailed, should be made. These are not only essential to catch filings and snippings, but save a vast amount of time. They catch tiny pieces when they fall, and in them the worker keeps the tools he is using constantly.

For small work it is convenient to have a jeweller's "side-light" for soldering at the right-hand side of each frame and skin.

The bench, as described and illustrated (Fig. 1), is better for all-round metal-work than the standard pattern jeweller's bench (Fig. 2). When using the former for large work or for repoussé, when one sits on

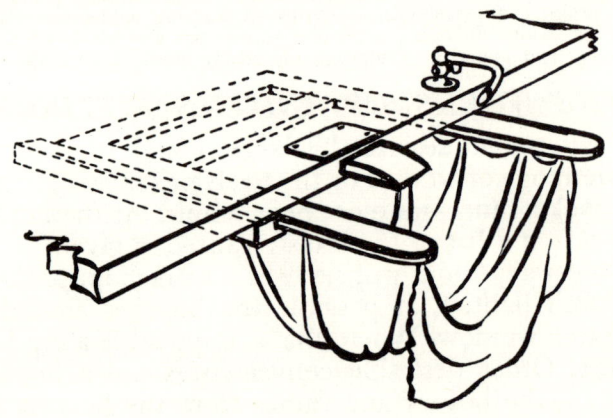

FIG. 1.—The ideal bench fitting for small work. The runners to which the skin is nailed are 1 ft. 9 in. apart.

a high stool, the slide can be pushed out of the way under the bench. It is very difficult to use a jeweller's bench for any work other than such as can be done while sitting on the low seat the jeweller uses.

The bench thus described is the ideal. If it be unattainable, any strong table or bench can be made to serve.

VICES AND ANVIL

The vice.—The ideal is a heavy "smith's leg vice," weighing 60 lb. or so, for each worker. This kind

THE METAL-WORKER'S TOOLS

of vice should be fixed immediately in front of the bench leg; sometimes the leg of the vice is secured to the wooden support. Firmness is the one essential. For hammered work the leg vice is far superior to the parallel bench vice. If this last-named kind only is available, it should be as heavy as possible. For filed work the parallel vice is perhaps the better one.

The anvil.—No matter what kind of metal-work we do, a smith's anvil, weighing perhaps 30 or 40 lb., is a great convenience. For rough work, however, any heavy piece of iron will serve. It is even possible to do much with an ordinary domestic flat-iron held face upwards in the vice.

THE FLAT DIE OR SURFACE PLATE

This should be of cast-iron —one 1 ft. × 1 ft. × 1 in. thick, planed flat on one side, is most useful. Something that will serve well can often be found on an engineer's scrap-heap. Here again the domestic iron is excellent for small work. For testing the truth of work a piece of thick plate-glass or a piece of thick wood or slate made perfectly flat will answer.

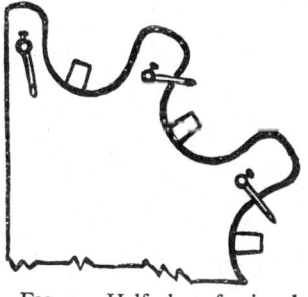

FIG. 2.—Half-plan of a jeweller's bench. Ideal for jewellery alone. Awkward for general work.

MANDRELS OR RING STAKES

These are, when large, 2 in. diameter and upwards, made from cast-iron. A useful size is one tapering from 8 in. to 2 in. and about 1 ft. 6 in. high. This should be turned smooth, but not polished. It is a truncated cone.

Below 2 in. diameter mandrels are usually called "triblets." These are best made from mild steel. One tapering from 2 in. to ½ in. and 1 ft. 3 in. long will serve nearly every purpose. Below ½ in. diameter they can be made easily, even without a lathe. Here again a scrap-heap will probably yield something useful.

HAMMERS AND MALLETS

Hammers.—For advanced work quite a number of hammers are needed, of varying shapes and sizes. Generally speaking, it is better to have light hammers rather than heavy ones : 4 oz. may be regarded as a standard. For our first exercises all we shall need are : a ball-pane hammer of the ordinary type, weighing 4 oz. ; a cross-pane hammer, also of the ordinary type, and of the same weight ; and a larger ball-pane hammer of from 10 to 14 oz.

Care should be taken, in selecting them, to see that the stails or handles are comfortable to the hand, and that the hammers " drop " well, that is, fall accurately, so that the centre of the face strikes the metal without conscious guidance.

A repoussé hammer of 2 or 3 oz. is also most desirable.

Mallets.—These are best made of boxwood—lignum-vitæ is not so close in the grain. A flat mallet, about 2 in. diameter, is a necessity. Larger and smaller ones are useful at times, as are also those with egg-shaped heads. For some purposes raw-hide mallets are good.

FILES

There are so many kinds of these that selection is sometimes difficult.

The *cuts* of files are : rough, bastard, second cut, smooth, and superfine. The *shapes* in common use are : *flat* ; *hand*—flat, with one edge left smooth, or safe ; *pillar*—long and narrow, safe-edged ; *half-round*—with one side flat and one rounded ; *round*, or rat tail ; *double half-round,* or crossing ; *square* ; *three-square,* or

THE METAL-WORKER'S TOOLS 17

triangular; *knife-edge*—one edge thick and one thin; *warding*—thin, flat, for filing the wards of keys.

The sizes.—Most of these shapes can be had from 14 in. or 16 in. long down to $4\frac{1}{2}$ in.

Very small files, all in one piece, known as *needle files*, are needed; 14 or 16 cm. are convenient sizes. They may be had in all the shapes mentioned, and in three different cuts.

For our first exercises we shall need: one 10-in. hand file, second cut; one 6-in. half-round, superfine; one needle file, flat, as rough as can be got.

It should be noted that *Sheffield* files are not so finely made as *Lancashire*. The latter are far better for fine accurate work. For rough work, especially for the quick filing of tools and punches, Sheffield files are excellent. Faulty files can sometimes be bought cheaply. These should be kept for work likely to injure a good file.

All files should be suitably and firmly handled. Avoid putting a small handle on a large file, and the reverse.

Rasps, file-shaped pieces of steel cut all over with spiky teeth, used for shaping wood, are necessary. They are cut in two grades—wood rasps and cabinet rasps. The latter are more generally useful to the metal-worker. Flat and half-round are both useful shapes, 9-in. or 10-in. a good size.

SHEARS, PLIERS, CORN TONGS, TONGS, HAND VICE

Shears.—These should be of good quality. A pair of straight tinman's snips, 10-in., a pair of jeweller's or dentist's shears, 6 in. long, and a pair of tinman's bent shears, 6-in. or 8-in., should be provided. If the worker is limited to one pair, 8-in. straight is the best size.

Nippers.—A small pair of Lancashire 5-in.

Pliers.—Of these we shall need one large pair. Electrician's combination pliers answer admirably. Besides these we shall need a smaller pair of flat-nose, 5-in., and a pair of 5-in. half-round snipe nose. Round nose can be added later. It is convenient to have three or four pairs that can be altered to any shape of nose we please. Usually the noses of ready-made pliers are too round.

For wire-drawing a pair of tongs is convenient and makes for quick working.

Corn tongs or tweezers.—These are simply forceps made of fairly stout steel. For our purpose we need a pair about $4\frac{1}{2}$ in. long made of steel about $\frac{1}{16}$ in. thick. The name seems to come from the fact that solder so often " corns "—melts into roundish beads.

Draw plates.—English or French. Round, square, oblong, half-round, etc.

A plate ranging from $\frac{3}{16}$ in. to $\frac{1}{64}$ in. diameter is advisable if not essential. For this range we may need two plates.

Light iron tongs, 9 in. or 12 in. long, made from $\frac{3}{16}$-in. or $\frac{1}{4}$-in. rod, are useful for soldering. A pair of forge tongs for holding small rods $\frac{1}{4}$ in. or so are also handy.

A small *hand vice*, Fig. 26, Lesson 3, is essential for making tools. If possible, a pair of slide pliers, vice-nose, should be included.

STAKES

These may be bought ready made, or we may make patterns, or models, in wood or plaster of Paris. We get these cast in malleable iron and file and polish them ourselves. A good size for the shanks or pegs which fit in the " crank," Fig. 3 ; or into the straight stake holder, is $\frac{3}{4}$ in. Figs. 4 and 5 show excellent shapes.

THE METAL-WORKER'S TOOLS

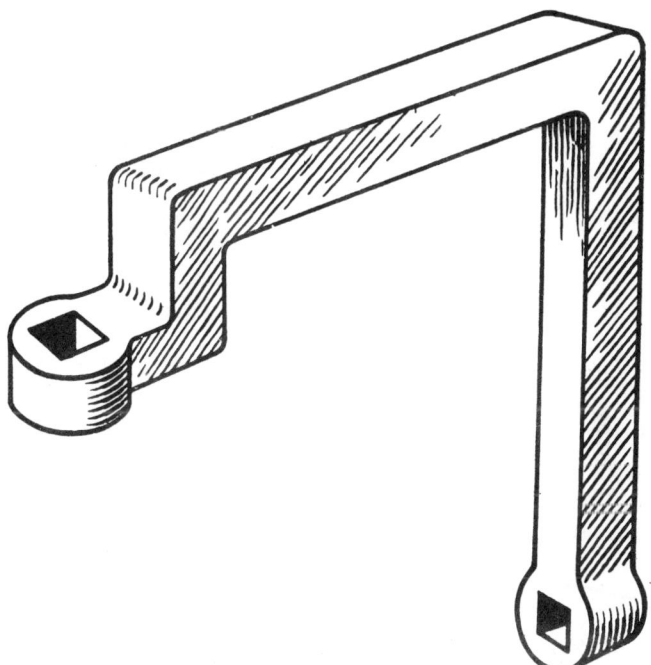

Fig. 3.—Made in wrought iron of about 1⅜ in. square. The holes are ¾ in.

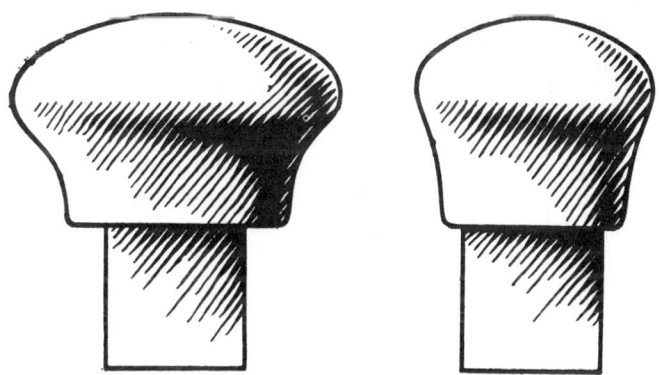

Fig. 4.—Side and end views ¾-in. shanks.

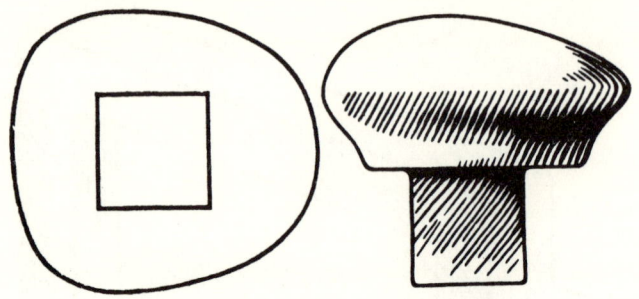

FIG. 5.—Plan and side view ¾-in. shank.

A "mushroom" or bottom stake with an 8-in. or 10-in. stem, Fig. 6, is essential; similar ones with different faces, e.g.—flat circular—will be needed later.

A "beck iron," though not essential, is useful—16 in. to 20 in. over all is a reasonable length.

DRILLS

In the absence of a lathe or a drilling machine, a side-wheel drill stock, "Millers Falls," American pattern, is excellent. The most useful sizes are those holding up to $1\frac{3}{16}$ in. and to $\frac{3}{8}$ in. The smaller one is all we shall need at first.

The actual drills we shall make normally from steel

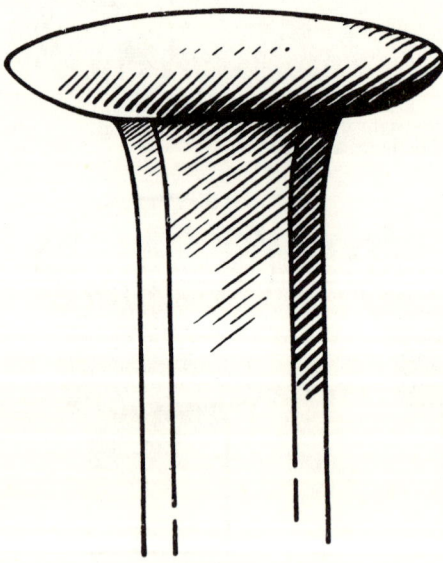

FIG. 6.

THE METAL-WORKER'S TOOLS

wire. For some purposes "twist" drills are better. Later on a jeweller's "pump" drill stock will be useful.

MEASURING APPLIANCES

We shall need:

A square.—"Stanley" 12-in. iron stock is excellent.

A rule.—"Chesterman" 12-in. divided on both edges, one $\frac{1}{16}$-in., the other from $\frac{1}{64}$ in. to $\frac{1}{8}$ in., is the most useful.

Pencil compasses.—A cheap strong pair.

Dividers.—"Starrett" 5-in. is the usual size: 3-in. are better for small work, and 7-in. for larger.

Scribing block.—A simple one is all we want.

A *standard wire gauge*, 1 to 35, or a *Birmingham metal gauge*, 1 to 24.

SAWS, ETC.

A piercing-saw frame which should take work 6 in. wide at least. Longer-armed ones, for wider work, are needed at times. The blades should preferably be round backed. No. 1 for fine work, No. 3 for ordinary, and No. 4 for thick metal are the most useful sizes.

A *back-saw* and blades are needed.

A *hack-saw* and blades, some coarse- and some fine-toothed, are also needed. Often it is more expeditious to saw metal than to chisel it.

A *scraper* can be made or bought.

A *set of gravers and scorpers*.

Oil-stone.—Any kind, so long as it is hard. "Arkansas" is perhaps the best.

A LATHE

Any plain lathe over $2\frac{1}{2}$-in. centre, foot or power.

SCREWING TACKLE

Screw-plate, or *stock and dies*, for screwing are needed. Those with loose dies from $\frac{1}{16}$ in., rising by $\frac{1}{32}$ in. to $\frac{1}{4}$ in., Whitworth thread, are generally useful. B.A. dies are also useful.

The taps taper, following, and plug, may be bought or made.

SOLDERING APPLIANCES

For soldering and annealing.—A hearth, if possible under a hood; this should be an iron or asbestos-

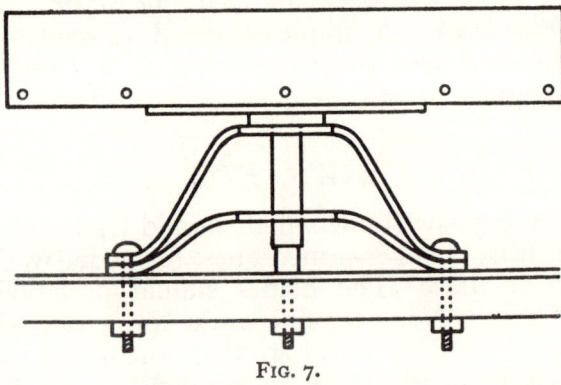

Fig. 7.

covered bench, upon which is bolted a revolving iron tray, at least 1 ft. 6 in. diameter inside and about 3 in. deep. Fig. 7 shows an efficient one of simple construction made of sheet and bar iron. It must turn easily but be quite free from wobble. The tripod support ensures this.

The tray is filled with coke broken into pieces of about 1 in. This is ideal for much; but for work that has to be kept flat, a 12-in. "Deflector" type fire brick, or similar pattern fire brick grooved on one side, is preferable.

THE METAL-WORKER'S TOOLS 23

Squares of thick iron wire gauze or net are also very useful.

Binding wire of soft iron, for fastening work together for soldering, is necessary. Nos. 18, 20, 22 for ordinary work, and No. 26 for very small work, all S.W.G., are convenient sizes.

Cotter-pins, $1\frac{1}{2} \times \frac{5}{32}$ in., are useful for cramping work, and a supply of $\frac{1}{8}$-in. iron wire for making cramps must also be provided.

Pickling appliances.—If possible a stout lead vat, burned at the corners, not soldered, fitted under a hood to carry fumes away, should be provided, together with a gas-ring for heating it. If this is not available, we must make shift with a large bowl or pan of earthen- or stone-ware. Pickle acts quite well when cold, but slowly. The vat should be placed so that any risk of splashing is reduced to a minimum.

Borax.—A slate to rub it on; any piece will serve, 6 in. square is a good size. A strong glass or earthenware pot is also needed for use with powdered borax.

Blowpipe and blower.—A blowpipe, Fletcher Russell, 8 C. No. 2 Type B, $\frac{1}{2}$-in. gas supply, or a Birmingham pattern of the same size; and a foot-blower, or bellows, of ample capacity, will serve for any work. These should be fitted with the best soft rubber flex obtainable. Metallic tubing is heavy, and, if allowed to kink, develops leaks. The gas-supply pipe should be on the large side, especially if it has to serve more than one hearth.

There is little to choose between the two types of blowpipe. The Birmingham type, with its lever control, needs a little practice to handle, but when mastered is certainly speedier than the Fletcher-Russell type. Its one defect is the absence of a valve to control the air supply. When using a foot-blower this makes no difference. One soon learns to do this effectively by greater or less pressure on the treadle of the bellows.

An ordinary mouth blowpipe.

A small "Bunsen"-burner is useful at times. Many solderings, difficult by other means, can be done with ease in a Bunsen flame.

PITCH POT AND BLOCKS

A pitch pot and a gas-ring for heating it. A "Negro" pot 9 in. diameter is a handy size. An ordinary plumber's *ladle*, $3\frac{1}{2}$ in. or 4 in. diameter, is needed. The join between handle and stem should be reinforced by riveting a stout iron strip over it. Unsupported, it will soon break.

Pitch blocks.—Squares of wood, almost any kind, 8 in. or 9 in. × 2 in. or 3 in., are very useful.

Pitch bowls.—Hemispherical bowls of thick cast-iron are better still: 7 in. or 8 in. is a good size. For these, *rings or collars*, made by sewing or riveting stout leather belting together, are needed for support.

LEAD LADLE

A plumber's ladle, 4 in. or $4\frac{1}{2}$ in. diameter, and a quantity of scrap lead should be provided.

POLISHING APPLIANCES

If available a spindle driven by foot or electric power is very welcome to the metal-worker. On it are used circular *brushes* of black bristle: some round, from 3 in. to 5 in. diameter, with two to four rows of bristles; some shaped like a circular hearth-brush; and some like a shaving-brush.

Mops.—Calico or soft leather discs to a thickness of $\frac{1}{2}$ in. to 1 in., riveted between stout leather discs, so that they will screw on the spindle, are used for the final polishings.

THE METAL-WORKER'S TOOLS

Hand polishing.—If the spindle is not available, the polishing must be done by using hand brushes. Black bristles of all sorts of shapes and sizes are to be had: 6×1 in. wide is a useful size. Sometimes small ones, approaching the size of a tooth-brush, are useful. Soft cloths and pieces of chamois leather are also wanted.

POLISHING MATERIALS

Emery cloth, No. 2, No. 1, FF, and No. 0 are all useful. " Blue-back," while more expensive than white, lasts much longer. Thin, oblong strips of wood covered with emery paper of varying grades, 000 being of almost incredible fineness, are very useful—these are of French make. They are useful, when worn out, for wrapping ordinary emery cloth or glass-paper around. The latter in its finer grades is excellent for very small, smooth work.

Powdered pumice.—This should be free from coarse particles. These may scratch badly. Also used in chaser's pitch.

Tripoli composition.—A fine earth, fragments of microscopic shells mixed with a thick grease.

Crocus.—A form of oxide of iron, in powder, or in composition.

Rouge.—Another form of iron oxide. Gives a lustrous finish but must be used sparingly.

Whitening—the ordinary commercial kind.

Water of Ayr Stone. A kind of slate to be had in pieces about 6 in. long from 1 in. to $\frac{1}{8}$ in. square. This gives a perfectly smooth surface.

OILS

Machine oil.—Any good brand.

Paraffin.—For removing thick grease, pitch, etc.

Tallow.—For a lubricant when drawing wire. Also used to make chaser's pitch.

Pitch.—Best brown Swedish. Must be pure, extremely tenacious, and of a distinct brown shade in certain lights.

SAND-BAGS AND STEADY BLOCK

Sand-bags.—For choice, circular leather ones, 8 in. or so in diameter, are best. Efficient ones may be made at home from some strong material, such as " ticking." These are good for resting pitch blocks upon.

Steady block.—A piece of tree-trunk—birch, elm, or other wood not too hard—about 18 in. diameter and 20 in. to 24 in. high.

CHEMICALS

First come the *fluxes* for soldering—*borax* for hard and " *killed spirit* " for soft.

Sulphuric acid, for pickling clean work that has been heated. It is used diluted. When cold, 1 part acid to 10 parts water ; when hot, the amount of water can be doubled or trebled. *Caution :* always add acid to water, never water to acid. The latter course is most dangerous. Beware of splashing acid or pickle on clothes.

Nitric acid.—For " dipping " brass, to remove all traces of oxide of copper.

Liver of sulphur.—For colouring copper, gilding metal, and silver.

Loam.—A soft, smooth, friable earth. When mixed into a thin paste with water is painted over soldered parts when the need for protection from heat arises. It is also used to prevent surfaces soldering together inadvertently.

CHAPTER III

SECTION 1

The hammering of metals—Raising.

THE HAMMERING OF METALS

WE have already noted very briefly the essential qualities of metals. Now we have to consider how the possession of these determines the methods and the tools of the craftsman in metal.

We saw that the primary outstanding quality is *malleability*, a word derived from the Latin for hammer.

We saw also that gold, the most malleable of all metals, was one of the first metals, if not actually the first, to be recognised as being metallic and different from all other substances.

When primitive man found that by beating a lump of native gold between two stones it would become wider and thinner, he made one of the great discoveries.

Further, when men, having found that a blow from a hard moving body could accomplish something that the entire strength of his body could never do ; and from this went on to find out that if the heavy hard body were fastened on a long handle, the force became greater, he took another very long step forward. Let us enact these discoveries by hammering a bit of lead, firstly between two stones, and then between a bright steel stake and a bright hammer face.

After the first experiment we shall notice that a print, an impression of any roughness, or texture, there may be on the stone appears on the thinned and widened lead.[1] After the second we shall see that the lead has become not only fine in texture, but in surface form also.

Under the hammer metal takes on something of Nature's own qualities. No longer is its surface as dead, lifeless, mechanical; it has become alive. We see, not one set rigid form, but one made, as Nature's are made, from a multiplicity of smaller ones, each contributing to the beauty of the whole.

A hammered form, or a hammered surface, provided it is genuine, is a perfect idiom in the metal-worker's language. It can be made to serve as a means of expression of our deepest thoughts.

The hammer is therefore the primary tool for metal-working.

Little wonder that the Blacksmiths' Company took as their motto, " By hammer and hand all arts do stand." The essential function of the hammer is to shape and, having shaped, to smooth.

The hammer may be well thought of, in action, as a tool that concentrates and intensifies force.

When a hammer is not sufficiently precise in its action, we interpose a punch between the hammer and the part or piece we wish to strike, and thus intensify the concentration of force still more.

On occasion, when a hammer used by hand is not accurate enough, and a punch would operate on too small an area, a tool known as a " swage " is used. This has a strong hinge, leaving stake and punch free to move in one direction only. Metal to be shaped is pushed between punch and stake while hammer blows rain down.

---

[1] Observation of this, coupled with the early use of seals, led straight to the stamping and pressing of metal into dies and matrices. Stamping has been used in all ages and by all races of metal-workers. It is not, as commonly thought, a peculiarly modern practice.

THE HAMMERING OF METALS

The practice of denting smooth metal deliberately with hammer marks is wholly evil. Where, in the course of working, the hammer leaves traces of its action, it is right to accept them, provided we use the hammer, as we should use every other tool, to produce the utmost possible accuracy and smoothness.

Of the two evils, affected roughness and mechanical smoothness, the first is the more deadly by far.

By using hammers of different forms, or by placing the metal to be struck on stakes or anvils of different forms, the metal can be made to lengthen, to widen, to become thinner or thicker; in short, to assume any shape we please.

When we use a wooden hammer, a " mallet " as we call it, the area upon which the impact operates is wider, and the effect less intense. This makes it the best tool to use when we wish to shape sheet metal without leaving any trace of the tool.

Just as, in using a file, we must never lose sight of it as a tool giving great precision of form, so we must also regard hammers and mallets. We must learn to use them so that their force is always applied to the right spot.

Good workmanship always accomplishes the greatest results in the smallest possible number of strokes.

Unfortunately, the term " beaten metal " is far too commonly understood to mean work done by thumping away with plenty of muscular, but very little mental, effort.

When using a hammer we must remember that, excepting for the delivery of very hard blows, we use the wrist only in striking. The tool must be held so that we are very sensitive to the direction of the blow, and the position of the head. We have to aim at striking with the centre of the face. This is clearly seen in Figs. 30, 31 (Lesson 7), and 40, 42 (Lesson 8).

Beginners have a tendency to strike with the edges. If clay be at hand, it might be well to flatten out a lump with a mallet, trying to avoid crescent-shaped marks.

The strength of the hammer blow is a matter of great moment. Usually the beginner hits too hard, for planishing the blow that would drive a small tack into soft wood is, normally, quite sufficient.

Sometimes, in the final stages, we give the hammer a kind of sliding motion, so as to spread the effect of the blow over a wider area.

So that we may the better understand the action of the hammer on metal, we should take pieces of metal and hammer them, some in one direction only, some equally in all directions, some unequally, and so on. We shall find that the metal will soon become hard and finally will crack.

We should also bend pieces of metal and flatten them again with a mallet until they crack.

These experiments should be varied, and the metal " annealed " or heated to redness after each course of hammering. Then we shall find the metal will stand much more hammering. (See under " Annealing.")

The different effects of compression and extension should be studied also.

Although metal can be worked with great freedom, there are limits which the worker must recognise. Hence the suggestion of these simple experiments.

One of the most difficult things to do is to make a sheet of metal lie perfectly flat and level. A note on the " buckling " and " setting " of metal will be found under Lesson 9.

The production of smooth surfaces on scraps of metal should also be practised. Try and try again until it is felt that to make the crescent " pecks " is more difficult than to hit truly.

As clear sight of each facet made by the hammer as

THE HAMMERING OF METALS

it falls is important, it is well either to anneal and pickle the metal clean, or to scour it well with emery cloth in one direction only. If the latter is done the hammer face is rubbed on emery cloth to make a slight grain. Then if the grain on metal is at right angles to that on the falling hammer, the mark of each blow will be seen distinctly.

The secrets of hammering are practice, use of wrist only, keeping the upper arm pressed against the body and the lower arm still, alertness to detect deviation from accuracy, and intentness on making the centre of the hammer face obey one's will—thought should direct every blow.

Fig. 8.—A flat hammer face. Note its deviation from the straight line.

Let us look at our hammers. First the ball-pane, 12 oz. or so in weight.

This will be used mainly for rough work—forging, striking chisels, etc. The face of this we shall leave untouched, and there will be no need to take any special care of it.

Of the others we must take the greatest care.

Fig. 8 shows on a large scale a side elevation of a flat hammer face. It will be noted that the word flat needs much qualification. The centre of an ordinary flat hammer $\frac{3}{4}$ in. diameter projects at least $\frac{1}{100}$ in. above the edges. When we buy our two small hammers we should take a sheet of No. 1 emery cloth, put a duster or some thick paper under it, and lay it on the bench. We should then rub our hammer face vigorously, slowly changing the direction of the strokes, and tilting the hammer slightly to every side so that the full face shown in Fig. 8 is produced. After the No. 1 emery cloth use FF., and finally No. 0, until something like a mirror face is produced.

Hammer faces must be carefully preserved from damp or acids which will rust them, and from use for striking hard steel or stone which will roughen them. They should, from time to time, be rubbed on a leather-covered board with a little oil and flour emery. When not in use, it is a good plan to smear oil over the bright faces.

The faces of neck hammers also should be rounded off and polished. No hammer is fit to use until its corners have been worn away by polishing. A hammer with a sharp angle, except for very special purposes, is like a bad-tempered person—a nuisance.

Mallets.—These too have to be made fit to use. The corners have to be well bevelled off to prevent splitting, splintering, and chipping. On a mallet with a $1\frac{3}{4}$-in. face, the bevel should be at least $\frac{3}{16}$ in. wide. One end of the mallet should be made as smooth as the smoothest file and glass-paper will make it. A rough mallet will leave its trace on smooth metal. The other end of the mallet is kept for general use (Fig. 9).

The foregoing applies with equal force to mallets that are shaped for raising. Beginners are very prone to treat them unfairly.

Hitting with the centre of the face is as necessary with mallets as with hammers.

RAISING

The photographs and illustrations to Lesson 8 should be looked at when reading the following. Instruction in the actual technique will be found there.

" Raising " is the process of shaping a vessel of some

RAISING

depth from a flat sheet. The term is used in one other craft at least. A " raised " pie is one with its walls and bottom made from one disc of paste.

In raising, the force is applied to the outside of the vessel; the metal is thus continually compressed. When we shape metal from within we speak of " doming," " dishing," or " bellying," and the metal is stretched. Often both processes are used in the fashioning of the same vessel. We have to use our judgment as to which is the better one to use for a particular job.

We are all familiar with the little crinkled moulds of paper used for baking cakes. A moment's thought will make it clear that it would be impossible to shape

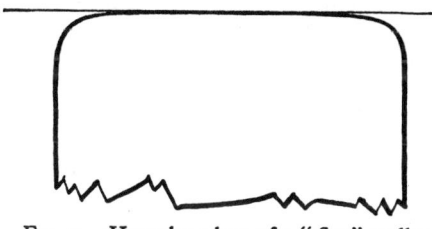

FIG. 9.—How the edges of a " flat " mallet should be rounded.

paper without crinkling, or creasing, it. If we take one of these moulds and flatten it out, we shall find that the diameter of the flat disc equals, exactly, the diameter of the base, plus twice the measurement of one side.

Let us think of a cylindrical vessel, say 2 in. diameter and 2 in. high. Its sides and base together measure 6 in. Shall we need a 6-in. disc to raise it from, and if not, how shall we find the right size to take ? If we were able to raise metal from a flat disc to a cylinder, without altering thickness in any way, we should need a disc equal in area to the superficial area of the vessel, roughly 15·72 sq. in., just under $4\frac{1}{2}$ in. diameter.

Four and a half inches diameter is amply large : a beginner would be almost certain to stretch the metal, and would produce a vessel perceptibly deeper than 2 in.

A good working rule is to take the average diameter of the vessel we wish to make, and to it add its depth. We use this first estimate as a starting-point. If we

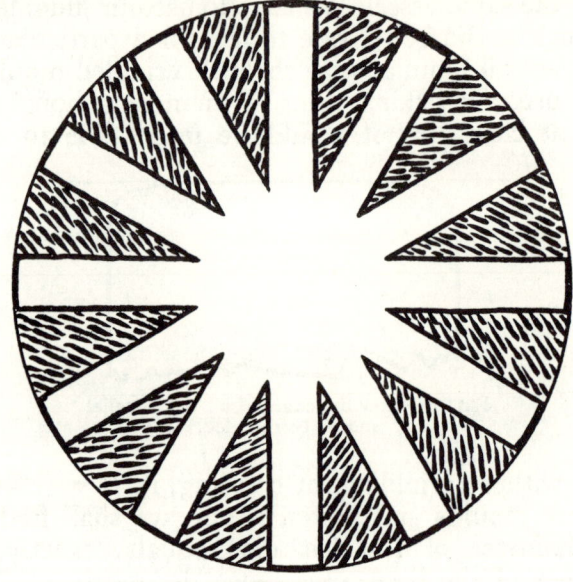

Fig. 10.

think the metal will not stretch—it tends to do so but slightly in vessels of convex outline—we add a certain amount, $\frac{1}{2}$ in. or $\frac{3}{4}$ in. in every 6 in. If the vessel we contemplate has much concavity, and in consequence we think the metal will stretch a good deal, we add nothing, or even reduce our estimate.

When we raise a vessel we make its sides or walls smooth. The creases and wrinkles that tend to form

RAISING

are straightened out under the mallet or hammer blows. This would, of course, be impossible if metal were not malleable. In raising we realise the metal's plasticity.

If we cut out the white part of the figure (Fig. 10), we could bend the parallel strips, solder the edges together, and thus form a cylindrical vessel 2 in. diameter and 2 in. deep (Fig. 11). If we were to take a metal disc the size of the whole circle, and raise it into a vessel of the same diameter, we should find that we get one 4 in. deep. The shaded triangles are equal in area to the parallel strips.

To understand clearly what happens when we raise, it is worth while actually to cut this figure out in thin sheet metal, and to beat it up with a mallet exactly as in the description of raising from the blank given in Lesson 8. Little effort will be wanted to raise the strips. When each strip forms part of a homogeneous disc, great effort is needed, so much, in fact, that, until we have found the knack of holding the metal against the blows of the mallet we shall do little but jar our left hand.

FIG. 11.—The circle of metal in Fig. 10 if raised would make a vessel of this depth.

When we bend the strips with the mallet we shall find that we have to aim our blows a little in front of the point where the metal is in contact with the head. In raising, the metal is, as it were, nipped or drawn in; not, as might be imagined, moulded over the stake. In raising with a hammer, especially, the strength of the blow[1] should be sufficient only to take the

[1] Until some degree of proficiency is reached, a mallet only should be used. A hammer in unskilful hands dents the metal badly.

portion of metal on which it falls down on to the head. If the blow is heavier than this, the metal will be stretched and thinned.

We should also confine our efforts to the simplest shapes. This will leave us free to concentrate on the actual work with mallet and stake.

CHAPTER III (*continued*)

SECTION 2

The heating and fusion of metals—Hardening and tempering steel—Annealing and pickling—Dipping.

THE HEATING AND FUSION OF METALS

BEFORE man could obtain mastery over metals he had two problems to solve. He had to obtain temperatures that would melt the more refractory metals, and he had to find out how to concentrate and apply heat to a small spot.

It would be noticed that fires burned more fiercely in a high wind, and that hot coals or embers would glow when blown upon. From this the deduction that a blast of air was essential would soon be made. Something like the familiar smith's hearth has existed from the most remote times, the only difference being that charcoal, not mineral coal, was used. Indeed, until little more than a hundred years ago the charcoal hearth and a flaring oil-flame were the only available sources of heat for soldering.

With the introduction of the easily controlled and applied gas-flame came the most revolutionary change the metal-worker had known since primitive times. In remote districts, where gas is not available, a satisfactory substitute can be found in the petrol or paraffin blow-lamp.

For small work a mouth blow-pipe with a spirit-lamp is quite efficient, even for hard soldering.

Soft Soldering.—Here another method of applying

the heat is available. A piece of copper, fitted in a long iron handle, can be heated and used to melt solder into joints and seams. This is the soldering " iron " or " bit."

The tip of the copper is always covered with a film of solder. When using a soldering-iron for the first time, the tip is filed bright while it is still hot, and is immediately dipped in the flux. A bit of scrap-metal, scraped bright, covered with flux, and with a tiny bit of soft solder in the middle, is put ready. The hot copper bit is rubbed to and fro until the solder melts and adheres. Each face is coated in turn with the bright solder. The soldering-iron is now said to be " tinned."

Through use and continuous, or excessive, heating, the film of solder disappears. It must then be tinned anew.

With a soldering-iron the heat can be localised to a degree impossible when a blow-pipe flame is used. It is, for instance, easy to hold many things in the hand while soldering in this way.

Applying the solder when using an iron.—A stick of solder may be held at the tip of the iron, or spots of solder may be melted off a thick piece and laid along the seam or join.

As the iron is moved along, the solder melts and flows neatly.

Soldering difficulties.—The aim of all good soldering is to make the solder melt, or flush, or run, exactly where we want it to go, filling up every crevice and join, but leaving a minimum to be removed afterwards.

The facts that metals expand with heat, and contract on cooling; in the case of a piece of metal that has been worked, the effects of expansion are to a slight but perceptible degree permanent; give rise to many of the difficulties of soldering.

HARDENING AND TEMPERING STEEL

With experience comes the power of realising what is going to happen, how trouble may be avoided, and how the effects of expansion can be countered.

Roughly speaking, the one thing to do is to heat the whole piece we are working on—bathe it in flame. This ensures even expansion and contraction.

When our work is partly of thick, and partly of thin, metal, the difficulties are much greater. Then we have, as best we can, to heat the thick parts more than the thin, so that all get hot together. Thin metal, of course, cools more quickly than thick, and we may have to continue heating the thinner parts for a while.

It was felt that, as soldering and brazing play such a large part in metal work, and that the many little variations and cautions, all of them important, that each job needs would be tiresome if put all together, these processes should be treated of in the course of those lessons. Notes on these processes may therefore be referred to in those places. See especially Lessons 7, 8, and 11.

HARDENING AND TEMPERING STEEL

The following notes may be found useful. Every job has its own problems: where these are in any way difficult, notes on them will be found in the lessons.

To harden a punch or chisel, we heat its point or edge, and about $\frac{1}{2}$ in. upwards, to redness in a fire, on a forge, or by a gas blow-pipe. Take care to cease heating before the steel begins to scale. While still glowing red it is plunged straight into cold water and moved rapidly about. The hardened part (chisels and punches are soft for the greater part of their length, otherwise they would be too brittle) should have a peculiar greyish look, and when touched with a file should prove so hard that the file will glance off with a ringing sound.

The chisel is now said to be "dead hard," and is far too brittle to use. Some degree of elasticity has to be restored, and this without destroying its hardness. This process is tempering.

Tempering is done by heating the steel again, but to a far lower temperature. The greater the heat the lower the temper: we judge the degree by watching the colour. This shows only on a bright surface.

The first thing in tempering is to polish the hardened part bright. Emery, a dark-coloured corundum—the same mineral as sapphires and rubies—is harder than hard steel; and the chisel will need only a little rubbing on the cloth to make it bright again.

For a first attempt at tempering a tool it may be well to apply the heat to the upper, striking, end, or to the centre of the chisel. If we use a blow-pipe flame, or Bunsen-burner, this is easily done. If we have only a fire, we can make a lump of iron or brick red-hot, and hold the chisel on it with tongs.

We must be careful to do our tempering in a suitable light. Then we shall see the bright white surface change colour.

First comes a very pale-yellow "*straw colour*"; this is the temper for tools to cut steel. This deepens to "*yellow*"—the temper for tools to cut iron and brass. The moment this colour is reached we plunge our chisel in the water again. Note that this applies to the actual edge and $\frac{1}{4}$ in. upwards only. Above that we shall see other colours in this order: "*yellow-brown*"— the temper for punches and tools that have no cutting edge. This deepens into "*brown*"—the temper for wood-working tools. Then the brown gives place to "*purple*" and finally to "*blue*." These last colours show the temper for springs and for large tools such as axes. Below "blue," steel is too soft to stand wear.

ANNEALING AND PICKLING

These facts should be copied out in tabular form and kept by the hearth.

ANNEALING AND PICKLING

When metals are worked to any extent they become hard, often so unyielding that further work is impossible. The molecules are in strain. If we heat, or " anneal," metal in this state—usually a low red heat is sufficient (there are, however, exceptions)—it becomes soft again. The strain is relieved.

When annealing, the heat should be applied, as far as possible, evenly all over our work. This lessens the danger of cracking through strains set up by unequal expansion.

With the exception of the precious metals group,[1] all metals absorb oxygen when heated in air, and a film of black oxide is formed. This can be scoured away with an abrasive, but the process is difficult, tedious, and endangers the surface of the metal. It is, however, easily removed by immersing the metal on which the black oxide—" scale "—has formed in sulphuric-acid pickle.

Some caution is needed in pickling work that has been silver soldered. The acid attacks the zinc in the solder freely, making it spongy and porous. The solder is said to have " fretted."

On removing an annealed piece of metal from the pickle, it will be seen that the black oxide has been attacked by the acid, and has been changed into a very finely divided metallic state. This is seen as a reddish film.

Immediately on removal from the pickle vat, the work should be washed in water (running, if available; if not, in several changes) and scrubbed vigorously

---

[1] Lesson 8 cautions the worker in silver that, in a strong light, silver shows little change in colour at high temperatures.

with a brush (a cheap nail-brush is admirable), using powdered pumice as an aid, until the metal is perfectly clean. After washing all traces of pumice away, the work should be dried, and we are ready to begin work again.

The best and most convenient way of drying a piece of metal is to put it into a box of saw-dust heated by hot water. This is usual in large well-equipped workshops, but would be a luxury in a small one or in a school.

For us the best thing is to blow a flame gently on our work until the water begins to steam. Then if put in cold saw-dust or rubbed with a rough absorbent towel our work will soon be thoroughly dry. The one thing to avoid is overheating; the oxide begins to form again quickly after the water has evaporated.

DIPPING

When working in copper alloys, brass, and gilding metal, it usually happens that reddish patches appear on the surface. The sulphuric acid in the pickle attacks zinc more readily than copper, but does so unevenly, hence these patches richer in copper than the yellower parts.

The colour of these metals is made even by dipping in dilute nitric acid—2 parts water to 1 part acid. The surface it produces is slightly rough, and if a bright finish is needed the metal must be polished again.

CHAPTER III (*continued*)

SECTION 3

Cutting metals—(*a*) By pressure—(*b*) By abrasion.

CUTTING METALS

Cutting tools.—Man's first conquest over Nature was won when he learned to make a tool with a cutting edge. Whatever craft we take, we shall find that the cutting implements take a first place. Certainly, before metal can be worked, some method of getting pieces of the size we need has to be found.

All cutting tools depend for their action on the edge of hard substance that will bite into the material to be cut.

Let us think of the various ways in which the edge, in our case almost always of hard steel, is made to cut.

Normally the unaided strength of the hand does not give sufficient force to cut quickly. We have to use some appliance that will help us.

Impact.—If we take a chisel we shall, even if it be small, and we press our hardest, be unable to make more than a tiny impression on the metal; but if we hit the chisel with a hammer, while the metal rests upon an anvil, or is held securely in a heavy vice, the edge will cut its way into the metal.

On a very small scale, using a tiny chisel and taking a small cut, we can cut metal by hand pressure. We call the chisels gravers or scorpers, and the act of using them engraving. When we use hammer and chisel we speak of chipping.

(a) BY PRESSURE

If we look at a pair of shears we shall see two edges, much more obtuse than chisels, and with two vertical faces in close contact, that can be moved with great force by leverage, so that a piece of metal placed between these edges has one part of it moved upwards, while the other is forced downwards, and is thus "sheared" in two. If we take a hard steel plate with an opening and fix it in an appliance that will allow us to bring down into the hole a piece of soft steel, fitting the opening exactly, we shall find that if we lay a piece of metal over the hole and bring the punch down, we shall shear out a disc, or other form, exactly the shape. This appliance is worked by a powerful screw, and is called a press. Though press work is outside the scope of this book, we shall have occasion to make use of "shearing" with a punch.

As with the other tools, it is well to practise accurate cutting with shears on bits of scrap-metal. The following should be noted :

Shears should be kept sharp. This is done by filing the narrow edges of the blades with an old steel file, or a carborundum file, so that an absolute angle is preserved. The rivet should be kept tight by an occasional tap with a hammer. Oil occasionally also. Whenever the shears show the least tendency to bend the metal, instead of cutting it, they need attention at once.

Shears should be used for cutting metal, not for wrenching it apart.

Metal up to 17 S.W.G., ·072 in. thick, can be cut by anyone having strong hands, if one limb of the shears be held in a vice. For a straight cut by the unaided hand 16 S.W.G., ·064 in. thick, is about the limit.

In a completely equipped workshop double-lever

CUTTING METALS

bench shears should be provided. These will cut metal up to 10 S.W.G.

A note on a simple and effective method of making small details with hammer and punch where the punch cuts with a shearing action will be found in Lesson 11.

(b) BY ABRASION

If we rub a coin on a bit of stone we notice that the coin loses a little of its substance in the form of dust, and that some of it clings to the stone.

From this it is evident that metals can be cut by abrasion. It would seem that the first files were stones.

Abrasion.—Speaking roughly, we may say that metal is abraded by a file, but that is not an accurate account of a file's action. If we take a bit of lead and scrape it with a pocket-knife, we shall see that the lead comes away in tiny shavings. With scrapers having much more obtuse edges, 60° or more, we can cut even hard metal. A " file " may be described as series of scrapers arranged in close order on one tool. A " float," a tool used by brass finishers for obtaining broad smooth surfaces, which is cut in one direction only (file cuts always cross each other) is even more accurately described in this way.

It should never be forgotten that a file is a cutting tool capable of the most precise work. It should never be thought of as something to be rubbed, in a careless haphazard way, over metal.

Strictly speaking, abrasion is only applicable to the action of a substance like pumice stone, emery cloth, " Water of Ayr " stone, and so on. Yet these, in their way, act in the manner of files.

Sawing.—A saw in its action has something of the chisel as well as the file.

Turning.—The difference between turning and other cutting operations is, of course, that the metal to be worked moves, while the tool is, by comparison, stationary. Here again is something of the chisel action. In fine cuts the tool works as a scraper, but with greater accuracy.

Drilling and screwing.—In both of these we get something of the action of the scraper and the chisel.

Filing.—We have already learned something of what a file is, and something of its action. Now we have actually to use it. The first thing is to stand properly. The work should be at the right height. This is that at which a file can be moved to and fro horizontally with the least effort. This will normally be found to be 2 in. or 3 in. below the level of the elbow when the arm is dropped straight down. In a school, wooden platforms of varying heights should be provided, so that each student may work easily.

If the student has never before used a file, he should lay it on a flat piece of wood fastened horizontally in the vice. He should then take the handle in his right hand : the end of this rests in the hollow of the lower part of the palm, between the masses at the base of the thumb and the outer side of the hand. The fingers are clasped around the handle, and the thumb is extended to its full length, straight out, and pressed tightly against the left side of the handle. The tip of the file itself rests in the same hollow of the left hand as that in which the end of the handle rests in the right (Fig. 12, facing p. 48).

If we now advance our left foot and throw our weight on it we shall find that we are in the best position to move the file horizontally.

It must be noted that a file cuts properly on the forward stroke only. On the return stroke we put no weight on it.

Before beginning to file metal, it is well to try on wood, until we find we can avoid rounding the edges.

CUTTING METALS

It is, in fact, excellent practice to make wooden models of tools, etc., on a big scale first, using a rasp for roughing out, and a file for finishing.

The skilled workman's brain, hands, and eyes are so trained that he makes his file move so as to leave a perfectly flat surface without apparent effort. It is claimed for some that by taking advantage of the curve of a file they can produce a slightly hollowed one.

It is not enough to file flat horizontally; we must be prepared to file in any plane we wish. We have, of

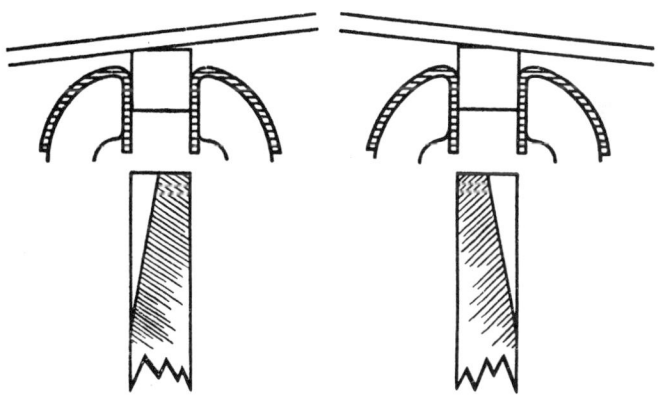

FIG. 13.—The shading shows the original face of the bar. The white triangles show the effect of filing in the wrong plane. Note clams of sheet metal.

course, to rely on our sight to a great extent, but we cannot look and see what every single file stroke has done. Here, the following will help.

Fig. 13 shows how we can tell if our file is not moving in the plane of the face of the bar. We notice the direction of the parting between the bright filing and the dark face of the bar. If it runs across at right angles we know we are right.

As soon as we have satisfied ourselves as to the accuracy of our filing, we have to think of the surface of our work. File marks are rarely good to look at, and usually the file has to move so many ways that our work tends to be patchy in colour.

The colour, grain, and texture of metal can be made even by " draw filing," and, as we shall see, the process is useful in another direction as well.

" Draw filing " is the putting of an even parallel grain, usually a fine one, on our work by holding the file at right angles to its length and rubbing it up and down, using some pressure.

Draw filing and ordinary filing leave distinct surfaces. If, therefore, we draw file a surface we can, just as with black steel, see if we have filed, or are filing, in the right plane.

When we come to file curved surfaces we have to remember that we are using a tool of precision. The difficulty here is to correlate properly the strokes of the file with the turning movement of the wrist.

In filing concave curves we may find a three-square, or narrow flat, file will give us better results than a half-round; the latter is usually too curved. For many purposes, a file of a pointed oval section, " crossing," is better than an ordinary half-round.

Large work is always held in a vice. " Clams " of metal or lead should always be used when a smooth surface is needed: vice-marks are very hard to remove.

Smaller work is held either in a hand-vice or on wood. Notches are cut to help us hold the work firmly against the file (Fig. 14).

Files need care. If at all greasy when bought they should be dipped in petrol, which is then burned off. Sometimes they are even heated in a gas-flame until their temper is lowered a little.

The great enemy of files is " clogging." Particles of metal adhere to the teeth of the file, preventing it from

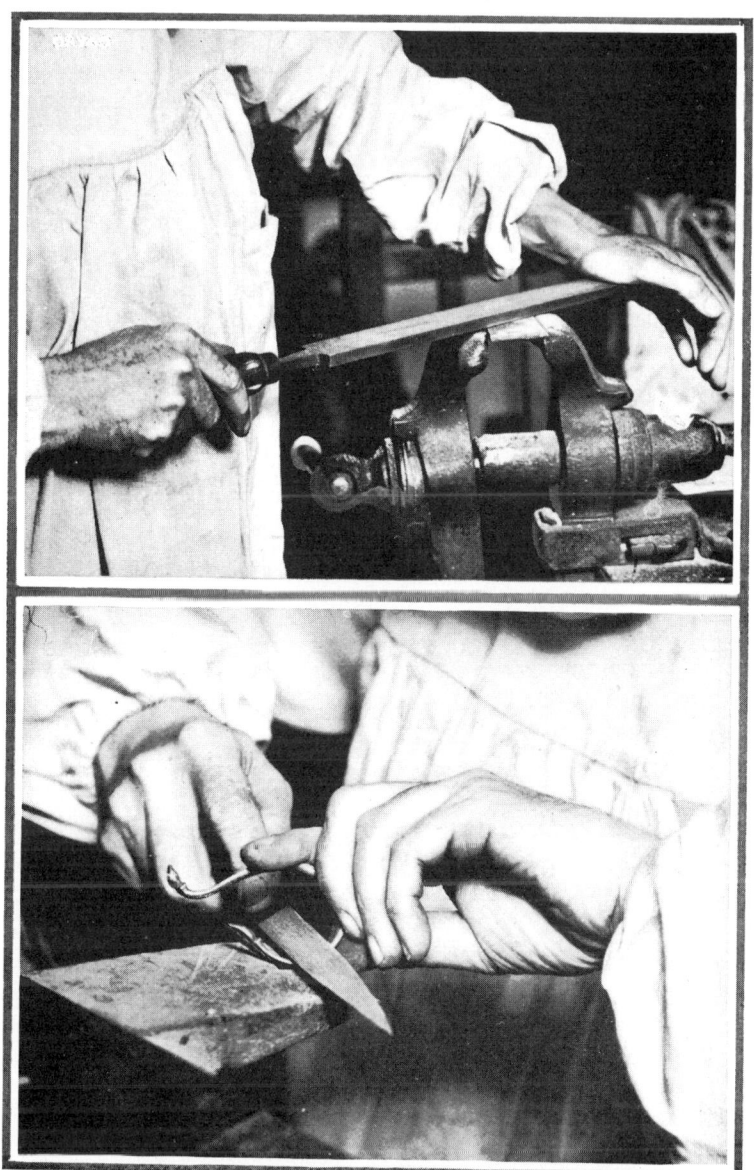

Above: FIG. 13. How to hold and use a flat file.
Below: FIG. 14.—Filing up a casting on the peg. Note the notch in which the cast handle is resting. The file is a 6-in. " smooth " half round one.

cutting, and making grooves in our work. Files should be cleaned regularly with a wire brush—" file-cleaning card "—and if any bits of metal do stick they should be struck off with a hammer and a brass punch. Sometimes chalk is rubbed on the file to prevent this clogging. The softer metals, copper and lead, etc., are the worst offenders.

When finally smoothing with a file the directions of the strokes should change continuously and cross and recross constantly. This prevents deep scratches from going unnoticed. When using other abrasives the same applies with equal force.

Emery cloth and glass-paper are used, as most convenient, in big and little pieces, flat and folded, in strip, and so on.

The French-made sticks of softwood covered with emery paper are useful, but in the coarser grades wear out quickly. They are then used with emery cloth wrapped around them. When preparing them a sharp point should be drawn along the back of the cloth in the angle between the wood and the cloth. This makes a sharp bend, and ensures that the cloth lies flat on the wood. As the surfaces wear, the cloth is torn off. One sheet used thus will last some time.

When a finer surface than emery cloth will give is needed, " Water of Ayr " stone is used. Stoning at first seems tedious, too tedious to be endured ; but as we go on we find it gives such wonderful results that we accept the task gladly. The soft stone can easily be made with a saw and file (use old ones) into any shape desired. It is used with water. The slime is wiped away as it forms.

In choosing stones remember that the spotted ones are coarser in grain than those of even colour.

CHAPTER III (*continued*)

SECTION 4

Drilling—Riveting—Wire drawing.

DRILLING

NORMALLY metal-workers, unless they are working in a fully equipped workshop, will make use either of a lathe, where the position of the drill is constant and the work is forced against it with the back centre, or a hand drill, usually of the geared side-wheel type; here the pressure is put on the drill itself.

Descriptions of the use of a drill will be found in other places—Lesson 5, etc.—but the following should be noted :

We must be able to drill holes exactly where we want them—not quite an easy thing to do. For this accurate centre punch marks are essential. We may at first fail to get even these quite rightly placed. It is always wise to give the centre punch a very slight tap first. Then if the tiny mark is seen to be wrong, another one may be struck close to it without difficulty. If the punch mark be deep before we notice the error, it can be corrected, to a degree, by inclining the punch and driving it towards the right place.

The direction of the drill is also most important: even in quite thin metal, say $\frac{1}{16}$ in., a drill, inclined but slightly, will make a hole a little out of position on the opposite side of the metal. We have to be careful to keep the drill perpendicular to the face of the metal we are drilling. Sometimes, of course, oblique drilling is a necessity, but will present no difficulty if the habit of drilling at right angles to the face of the metal is formed. Remember that one has to look two ways to ensure right direction.

Usually it is the last little distance that is troublesome to drill. Some metals clog and take on a hard burnished surface at the bottom of the hole. At this stage the drill often needs sharpening. Do not put much pressure on as the drill is coming through : the thin end is likely to stick and break.

When drilling two or three pieces of metal with a series of holes to be spaced identically on each, it is as well to clamp them in the vice, in a hand vice, or to fasten them—" tack "—with a speck of soft solder.

If, after all our trouble, we find that holes which were intended to be perfectly spaced are not so, they can be regulated by the use of the tip of a round needle file. The hole may be led, or drawn, towards the right spot.

If we have to enlarge holes, a clock-maker's broach or reamer is useful. Very efficient ones can be made by tapering down a piece of $\frac{1}{8}$-in. or $\frac{5}{32}$-in. square steel. Broaches are easily broken. Beware of letting them get stuck fast.

RIVETING

When we speak of metals as malleable we imply that they are plastic. They may be extended by hammer blows and they may be compressed.

Is it not more than probable that some primitive metal-worker found that a short length of metal rod would shorten, expand, and spread out at the ends under repeated hammer blows ? This fact observed, the attempt to join pieces of metal together by drilling holes and fastening them together by passing a short rod through and hammering it so as to spread the ends out would follow inevitably. This is riveting—one of the most important of metal processes.

Fig. 15 A's show the simplest form of riveting, with the rivets made of simple short lengths of wire. The one difficulty in using these is the keeping the lower face of the two pieces we are riveting at the proper distance above the flat die on which the rivet itself is resting. A secondary difficulty, which applies to other

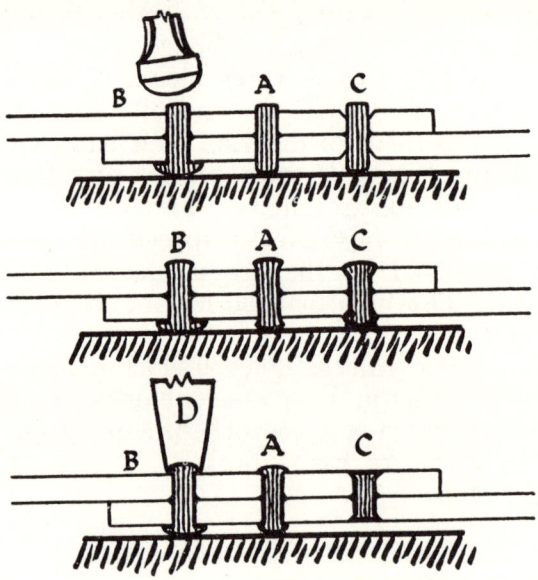

FIG. 15.

forms also, is the leaving of exactly the right length of rivet projecting above the surface in all cases, and when we are using simple lengths of wire below as well.

Fig. 15 B's show the easiest and best form of riveting, whenever the right size of headed rivet can be got, and when there is no objection to the presence of the head.

RIVETING

Fig. 15 C's show how two plates may be securely riveted together without any projection. The two outer ends of the holes are countersunk to a fair depth. The rivet head as it is driven down (this is done from both sides) fills up the depressions completely. If well done the rounded rivet ends fill the space so well that when filed off flush they are practically invisible.

It will be noticed that the hammer head, shown at B in the upper figure, is well rounded, and that it is directed a little away from the central line. The point of impact should travel in circles all around the rivet, the centre receiving but very few blows. Care must, of course, be taken that the hammer falls on the rivet head only. Dents and bruises around a rivet head, obviously the result of unskilfulness, are very annoying.

Fig. 15 D shows how the hammered end of a rivet is shaped and smoothed with a hollow-ended round punch.

It is well to countersink, or chamfer, the edges of the holes where the two plates come in contact, especially if the rivet fits tightly in the hole.

It is important that the size of the rivet and the drill used for the holes be properly related. The rivet should push in with ease, but be sufficiently tight to stay in the hole unsupported.

The amount to be left projecting (the importance of this has just been noted) varies considerably: if a large expanded head is wanted more must be left, and so on.

It is seldom that rivets of exactly the right length can be bought. The surplus is cut off with the nippers, and if the job is in any way particular, it must be levelled with a file. For very exact work a bit of steel of the right thickness with a hole in it should be used and the rivet filed off flush with it.

Such things as feet for boxes, etc., are often riveted on conveniently, a peg being left on for that purpose. If it is desired that a knob, for instance, be riveted on in such a way that it cannot be turned round even when great force is used, the hole itself and the lower end of the countersink are notched with a needle file. The riveting drives the metal into these, making the knob perfectly secure.

In cases where damage would result from the foot or knob resting on unyielding steel while being riveted, lead should be put between. If the piece be so thin as to make this impossible, it may be safely gripped in thick $\frac{1}{4}$-in. lead vice clams.

The applications of riveting are endless. The holes and the rivets, especially if they be in one piece with the part to be riveted, when they are called lugs, may be of any shape. On a large scale tubular rivets are often met with. The hollow stem of a cast-brass candlestick may have projections to attach it to base and grease-pan by riveting.

If rivets have to be removed, the projections must of course be filed off flush. If, when this is done, they are difficult to locate, heating the piece will probably make them visible. When driving a rivet out use a flat-ended punch, very little smaller than the rivet, so as to avoid expanding its end. The opposite end to that struck may be placed on lead or softwood until it projects sufficiently. Then a flat die with a hole in it is better. Do not try to drive rivets out unless the metal is well supported.

Rivets should, normally, be annealed soft before using. Ordinary brass " escutcheon pins," to be got anywhere, are often convenient. If too hard anneal them.

WIRE DRAWING

Metals are ductile.—We have already noted this briefly ; here are notes on the actual process which this property makes possible.

WIRE DRAWING

From the account given in Exodus of the making of the Jewish tabernacle, it is clear that the first wires were made by cutting up sheets of metal into narrow strips; these were worked into fabrics. These strips inevitably must have been used in very early times, for threading beads of precious stones upon. Difficult as it may seem, the art of drilling small holes through hard stone was practised in the most remote times. Soon it must have been noticed that when a strip of gold had been pulled through a hole in a stone it became longer, and in section, the exact shape of the hole. Thus was discovered the ductility of metals.

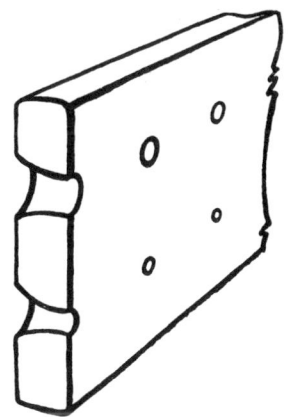

FIG. 16.—A round draw plate.

The process of making wire by pulling a strip of metal through a hole in a plate of hard steel we call "wire drawing." Fig. 16 shows a section of a round draw plate. The name of the section of wire produced is given to the plate, round, square, etc.

Wires of $\frac{1}{8}$ in. or less can be pulled by hand, the plate being held in the vice.

Fig. 17, A and B show the pointing of wires. A is on right lines—a long gentle taper. B is wrong—

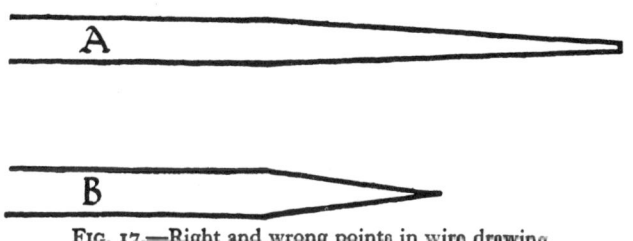

FIG. 17.—Right and wrong points in wire drawing.

a short taper coming to a fine point. If we attempted to draw a wire pointed thus the end would keep on breaking off.

We put the point of the wire through the hole we deem right, and taking a firm grip of it with draw tongs or large pliers, pull it until we have a fair length projecting : 1 in. is not too much for large wires, $\frac{1}{2}$ in. for medium, and $\frac{1}{4}$ in. for fine wires. Then, if we can, we pull the wire steadily through the plate. If we find we have chosen too small a hole we try a larger one. A little oil should be used.

The wire is then drawn through the hole next smaller in size, and so on, until it hardens to such a degree that we can pull no more. It is then coiled up carefully and evenly and annealed. This is a most important point. If any loose loops or ends are exposed to the action of the flame they will certainly melt. When wires are fine, 21 S.W.G. and less, it is well for beginners to bind their coils of wire tightly round with iron binding wire while annealing. The pad of tangled iron wire, advised for soldering in Lesson 10, is best to rest wire on for annealing. (See Fig. 51, p. 113.)

To sum up. Make long gently tapering points, not too thin at the tip. Do not put too much force on until a reasonable amount of wire is held in the tongs. Use the greatest care in annealing.

Wires have a peculiar smoothness of quality all their own. Whenever we make use of them we must keep this charm unspoiled as far as we possibly can.

Experiments in the amount of working of wires, by drawing, or bending, with and without annealing, should be made, so that the worker may gain a knowledge of what may be done safely.

Everyone has at one or other time in their life amused himself or herself by twisting and plaiting threads or strings of all sorts together. The possibility

WIRE DRAWING

of treating wires in the same way was of course realised in the very dawn of metal-working. The use of corded, or twisted, and plaited wires is, and has ever been, universal.

For first experiments in twisting wire a little windlass made out of a bit of hard-drawn wire and a strip of metal (Fig. 18) is excellent. A hook put in the side wheel-drill stock is speedier, but not so safe.

Let us draw some wire, metal, or silver, to three different sizes, say 26, 22, and 20 S.W.G., and try the effect of twisting.

One of the most useful effects is to be got by twisting two wires to the right and putting them side by side

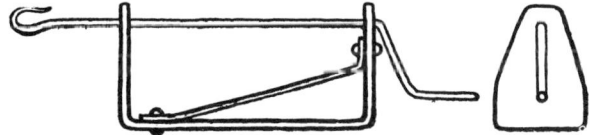

FIG. 18.—A useful appliance for twisting wires.

with two wires of identical size twisted in the left-hand direction.

Corded or twisted wires may be subjected to further treatment. A loose twist flattened under the hammer is very delightful. Tight cords pulled through drawplates of various sections also take on different qualities, often most useful.

Wires to be twisted need annealing with the greatest care and evenness. If, when we twist wires, we find a cord is forming that is uneven, we must anneal the parts that are loose and twist again until it is even from end to end.

Close and careful coiling is of course the great secret of even annealing. It is easy to see when a close coil is annealed properly. The need for extreme skill in manipulating the blow pipe flame is not so essential.

CHAPTER III (*continued*)

SECTION 5

Polishing and finishing—Metal colouring—Silver-plating.

POLISHING AND FINISHING

CERTAIN directions about polishing are given in the lessons; but we need to have some idea of the principles of polishing so that we know what to aim at.

The lustre of metals is one of their chief beauties.

There are, of course, times when metals must be left dull. Large wrought-iron work, and some castings in bronze, would obviously be wrong if they were highly polished.

Nearly always, however, metal on a small scale, such as we deal with in this book, is properly bright.

Bright polishes can easily be carried to excess. The ordinary silver seen in retail shops, for instance, could not possibly retain its dazzling whiteness in use; but the soft lustre of fine old silver-work, well cleaned, is entirely delightful.

The good metal craftsman tries to reduce the polishing needed on his work to a minimum. Whatever tool or process we use unskilfully, clumsily, unintelligently, will inflict damage. Hammers peck, bruise, dent. Files gash and scratch. Solder can blob, spread, obliterate form. Each operation should be as perfect and complete in itself as we can make it. Nothing should be left on the chance that it will come right at the next stage.

Despite the utmost care we take, some scratches and

POLISHING AND FINISHING 59

blemishes will reveal themselves when we begin to polish.

In the happier times, when men were craftsmen, indeed, before the subdivision of labour became a menace, each man enjoyed the fruit of his work. Then the knowledge that carelessness and lack of skill would have to be paid for by hours of laborious hand polishing made bad work too costly. Useful and necessary as a power-driven spindle is to the metal-worker, it has, nevertheless, been one of the most potent causes of the decay of craftsmanship.

What sort of surface finish are we to aim at?

The only rule we can lay down is that it should be one that displays the beauties of our work to the utmost, and that can be maintained with a reasonable amount of cleaning.

Many polishing materials, although they make metals quite smooth, leave them dull. Lustre-raising materials act very differently, and bring out this peculiar quality.

To the trade worker, polishing means the smoothing process. Finishing is applied to the final raising of the lustre. In this book these words have this significance.

The polisher for the trade silversmith and metal-worker uses circular discs—" bobs " of felt or leather of varying sizes, from 1 in. to 1 ft. or more in diameter, rotated at a high speed, 1,000 to 2,000 revolutions a minute, on a power-driven spindle. A tray with high back and sides covered to make a hood over the bob contains a fine but fast-cutting abrasive " Trent sand." The work is held by both hands against the bob, and from the palm of the right hand sand is fed between the metal and the bob. For professional polishers this is doubtless the best method, but is too arduous and dangerous for others.

Here is the order of the polishing processes normally

followed : All filed parts are emery clothed—use No. 1 or FF according to the scale of the work, or the grade of the last file used : FF is the most generally useful. If a very fine high polish is needed FF may be followed by O. The making and use of " emery sticks " has already been noted. In whatever form, the strokes of emery cloth, as indeed of all abrasives, must continually cross and recross.

The emery cloth is followed by " Water of Ayr " stone : this is especially useful for such parts of the work as cannot be reached by other means.

The next appliances we need are brushes (if we have a spindle, even one driven by foot power, we shall find it of the greatest use)—circular for the lathe spindle, and flat if we have to use them by hand : cheap nail-brushes are quite good.

The brush used vigorously and intelligently (the aim being to subject hollows and projections alike to its action) will soon give us the smooth even surface we need.

Fine pumice powder and oil mixed into a thick paste is as good a material as we can get, being cleaner than " crocus "—a red iron oxide.

Polishing the inside of a bowl, a box, or a cup is a difficult matter to do by hand. For the lathe " end," brushes and mops are procurable. These may be used by hand if a tedious and strenuous job is faced.

After using pumice and oil all traces of it must be removed by wiping and, finally, washing with hot soda-water to remove grease and grit.

Well-polished work can be made bright and lustrous very quickly, and with little effort by brushing with Tripoli composition and a little paraffin. After washing, a vigorous rubbing or brushing with a soft brush, or cloth, and chalk will give a fine soft polish.

A good metal-polish is often most useful.

Washing in hot water with a good soap powder will often clean metal without disturbing the colour that comes naturally and is so very charming. This would seem to be not generally known.

METAL COLOURING

One of the beauties of metal is that, with age, and under certain conditions, it takes on fine surface colour —" patina."

Usually this is the result of the action of sulphur in the atmosphere, or acids of the earth in the case of buried metal.

Metals, especially copper and its alloys, that receive constant handling and rubbing, develop a surface that, in a way, acts as a protective skin.

These colours can be produced artificially. An excellent account of the processes and many recipes are to be found in " *Silver-work and Jewellery*," by Henry Wilson (Pitman).

The most easily used colouring solution is made by dropping a small lump of " potassium sulphide "— " liver of sulphur " —into hot water. This is rubbed on to the surface of the clean metal with a " dabber " —a thin stick with a pad of soft rag tied on one end. A little powdered pumice—fine—is used so that the solution acts directly on the metal. The pumice rubs away any greasy film that may come from one's fingers. Some little practice may be needed before an even surface can be got.

After all traces of sulphur are washed away, the work is dried carefully, and is finally rubbed over with a very little floor or furniture polish—beeswax and turpentine is good. This puts a film, impervious to the atmosphere, upon it, and so prevents further change.

Metals coloured by sulphur are often, but wrongly, said to be " oxidised." The term is clearly wrong, especially when used of silver, a metal not acted upon by oxygen, but very susceptible to sulphur. Liver of sulphur is admirable for silver.

Copper and its alloys will often take on a fine colour when heated until the oxide begins to form. A perfectly clean bowl held in a gas-flame and rubbed hard at intervals, while still hot, but not hot enough to scorch, with a clean soft rag, will often take on a fine and lasting colour.

Metal should be rubbed at fairly frequent intervals, even when there is no thought of making it bright. Friction acts as a deterrent of corrosion.

SILVER-PLATING

It often happens that when we have made a piece of work in metal we wish that it were in silver. Here electro-plating comes in to help us. If the following instructions are followed we shall have a piece of work that will not only look very like silver, but will wear for many years, if treated properly. Frequent washing will obviate the too-frequent use of powder, paste, or liquid.

Firstly, a piece to be silver-plated should be wrought and polished with as much care as if it were actually silver. This applies to the outside of a vessel. The inside may safely be left to the electro-platers.

Secondly, a reasonable amount of silver must be deposited. On a piece about 5 in. diameter and 2 in. deep—say one with a superficial area of 100 sq. in., or thereabouts, at least 1 oz. of silver is necessary. If less than this, although the work will look right for a time, it will not stand up to ordinary wear and tear.

The cost of plating a vessel of the size named above with 1 oz. of silver, together with the charge for polishing the inside, should be, roughly, 10s. The order sent to the electro-plating firm should run as follows:

SILVER PLATING

"Polish —— inside only, do not touch outside.

"Silver-plate (here specify weight or cost—say 1 oz. or 10s., or whatever we wish). Finish bright inside only. Outside to be left as it comes from vat."

When we get our work from the platers we make a very hot, but weak,[1] solution of liver of sulphur; and we should have an ample supply of boiling water available.

Then with the dabber, no pumice is needed for silver or plated work—we apply the solution to the frosted electro-plated surface as evenly and quickly as possible, until it turns various shades of blue, purple, and grey. Plated work must not be allowed to go black. The inside may be coloured or not, in any case it should be done lightly.

The instant the right colour is reached the whole is washed in running water. After that in hot water with a soft brush and soap. Finally, it is rinsed in the hottest water possible, and dried on a clean soft towel.

The work is now rubbed up with Tripoli composition, moistened with paraffin,[2] using a soft brush (an old tooth-brush perhaps), or a bit of cotton-wool until a soft silvery colour is reached. Next take soft rag or cotton-wool, and rub vigorously until the lustre comes up.

Wash again in hot water, using soap powder, and after rinsing and drying (use hot water again) it may be rubbed up as brightly as desired with a chamois leather, a soft cloth with a very, very, little rouge.

The whole should now have a delightful colour and finish, not unlike that of a well-kept piece of old silver.

[1] A bit as large as a hazel-nut in a pint of water will be about right.
[2] A good metal-polish is almost, if not quite, as good.

CHAPTER III (*continued*)
SECTION 6
Piercing.

PIERCING

METAL is pierced by pressing, a shearing action; by drilling and filing, when holes far removed from the round, are only to be made laboriously; and by sawing with a very thin and fine saw: this last with its ease, its speed, its almost illimitable range, is the most generally useful.

We have noted the frame and the saws in Chapter II. Here are a few notes on the use of these tools.

Before we begin we need a saw peg. This is about 8 in. long, 3 in. wide, with a V-shaped notch, about 2 in. wide and $2\frac{1}{2}$ in. deep, or thereabouts, cut in one end. The peg may be held in the vice or screwed to the bench. The one point essential is that it should project so far beyond any obstruction that the hand underneath—as it moves the saw up and down—shall touch nothing.

When we look carefully at a piercing saw we see that the cut it will make will be but a very little wider than the saw itself; and that the distance from the front of a tooth to the back of the saw is always a little more than its width. From this it is clear that, although the saw can be made to follow curves, it cannot be turned around in the slot. Yet, unless we can make the saw turn in a very small compass its range will be too limited to be of much use.

Above: FIG. 20.—Using the saw frame. (See footnote on page 66.)
Below: PLATE II.—Horse Brass (Modern), and Clock Fret (English, early eighteenth century). (See Chapter VI.)

PIERCING

The secret is that the saw is kept constantly in motion, and the turning movement is made with little force, so that the up-and-down stroke is never checked. The saw thus cuts away a tiny, but sufficient, space for it to turn in without breaking.

It is, of course, obvious that before we can cut even one hole in a bit of metal, we have first to make a hole to pass the saw through. Drilling is the only thing if the metal be thick, 21 S.W.G. or more. Thinner metal may be pierced with a punch. Fig. 19 shows an efficient one, made from $\frac{3}{16}$-in. steel about 2 in. long. The plate to be pierced is laid on a lead cake, about $\frac{1}{2}$ in. thick. The rough edges made by the punch as it comes through are filed away. Then, if the metal is still too uneven to work well, it should be malleted flat, gently.

Fig. 19.—Piercing punch.

For a preliminary practice take some bits of scrap-metal, 20 S.W.G. or thinner, and upon them mark with scriber, dividers, and rule a series of small, about $\frac{1}{2}$-in., circles, squares, triangles, etc., and drill or punch a hole as close to the line as is consistent with safety.

Take the frame and a No. 3 saw. Screw the saw firmly in the upper jaws (avoid using pliers, too much force tends to strip the thread of the screws) with its teeth pointing downwards.[1] Pass the saw through the hole in the metal (see that the marked side is uppermost), rest the upper end of the frame against the bench, press the body against the handle to get the right tension, and screw the saw tightly in the lower jaws. The tension should vary with the size of the saw. A rough guide is to hang the frame on the finger,

[1] This means that the saw, in its action, presses the metal down on to the peg.

66   A FIRST BOOK OF METAL-WORK

by the saw; if the saw bends slightly it is right. A too loose saw is a nuisance; it should be taut.

Study Fig. 20,[1] and hold saw frame and metal as shown there. Grip the handle of the frame loosely but sensitively. Lift it up as high as it will go. Hold the metal on to the peg with the tips of the fingers of the left hand. Take care to have the line, to which we are to cut, between the eye and the saw; this enables us to see clearly that it is cutting rightly. Now with a firm but gentle stroke pull the saw downwards, giving the least possible pressure forward: we shall find the saw begin to cut. When we have reached the line[2] we turn the metal (wherever possible the metal, rather than the saw, is turned) and saw along the line. As the dust from the saw accumulates it is blown away. When we come to a corner we may find it a help if we let the saw ride against the wood while we wriggle out the hole for turning the saw. Continue these exercises until we can cut these simple shapes with fair accuracy.

Points essential to success are: the saw must move as nearly as possible in a vertical line—beginners always forget to have their right hands far enough under the peg; the movements of the saw and the metal must be so correlated that the saw moves in even, sweeping curves, and does not stick; the line must be followed as closely as possible but must not be cut away—once this happens our difficulties are increased many-fold.

Piercing saws, being of hardened and tempered steel, are very brittle. Some, even in the hands of professionals, snap in a few seconds. Although we may

---

[1] Note the slot: the saw peg is held in a vice; note that the metal is held on the peg by the finger-tips only. The saw is actually nearer the vertical than the photograph shows.

[2] The hole should be drilled as close to the line as possible, so long as it does not destroy it.

PIERCING

measure our skill by the number of saws we use, we must not be discouraged unduly when they break.

At first we shall find that our piercings will need some truing up with needle files; but we must aim at reaching a standard where this is unnecessary.

A piece of beeswax should be used as a lubricant for the saw. Rub it up and down the blade occasionally.

The patterns for saw piercing may be drawn directly on the metal, and for simple geometrical patterns, where extreme accuracy is essential, this is best. Normally, the most convenient way is to make a tracing on thin paper and paste on the metal.

Where numbers of the same pattern are to be cut, one pattern is cut as perfectly as possible, smeared thinly with printer's ink, and prints taken from it on thin paper. These are pasted on the metal.

We have already noted that the saw must move vertically. If we allow it to slope we shall break many saws. We shall also find, when cutting metal of any thickness, that the back will differ very considerably from the front.

The height of the seat is important. As the worker sits at work with his upper arm vertical, the lower arm and hand should be horizontal, and at the top of the stroke.

CHAPTER IV

THE LESSONS

Introductory—Lesson 1. Chisel—Lesson 2. Plate (cutting)—Lesson 3. Centre punch—Lesson 4. Scriber—Lesson 5. Drills—Lesson 6. Escutcheon from 2.—Lesson 7. Dish or Tray—Lesson 8. Raising, Hammering and Mounting a Bowl—Lesson 9. Cigarette Box—Lesson 10. Circular Box with Lid—Lesson 11. Serviette Ring—Lesson 12. Tea-pot Stand.

INTRODUCTORY

THE impulse to make something complete in itself at the very beginning of a craft education is perfectly natural and, so far, perfectly right. On the other hand, the young student is often prone to overlook the need for discipline of hand and eye before he can tackle even simple things quite successfully.

The lessons that follow, if carefully and intelligently worked, will take the student to a point where he can look ahead without being disheartened by the difficulties of more advanced work. They provide a series of exercises chosen for their value in the building up of a sound technical knowledge.

The ideal the writer has kept in mind is that the student shall acquire a technique adequate to express his personality in terms of metal.

The lessons are to be regarded as practical exemplars of the grammar of the craft. Now, a knowledge of the grammar of a language does not of itself ensure good speech, or writing, yet a good speaker and writer obeys the laws of grammar, but instinctively rather than consciously.

A gentleman, though he obeys the rules of etiquette, does so, not because he knows them by heart, but because he expresses the kindness and gentleness that are inborn and bred in him.

SIX PRELIMINARY LESSONS

The problem that every artist and craftsman has to solve for himself is how to find freedom within the law ; how to use his inventive faculties to their fullest while keeping a firm hold on the principles of sound craftsmanship. This way, and no other, leads to " perfect freedom."

It should be clearly understood that the drawings in this book are not intended as copies. They are merely guide-posts pointing to paths which will lead to the making of pleasant things, sound in design and workmanship.

It may sometimes, perhaps often, happen that the student is already perfectly familiar with a tool, the use of which is described at length in the exercise he wishes to work out. He should, of course, feel at perfect liberty to alter his procedure as he thinks best. Rarely is there one way, and one way only, of doing a job. Some students will probably, and rightly, wish to alter the sequence of the lessons.

The student who really wishes to become a competent workman must not be afraid of some amount of comparatively dull, uninteresting work. Accurate filing and polishing are not always exciting ; yet upon them depend much of the charm and beauty of fine work. It is, in truth, a matter of the highest moment that tasks of this kind be taken in the right way. If our desires for excellence and beauty are keen enough, we shall count the effort as a small price to pay for the intense joy of the craftsman when he has achieved them.

It will be found that the methods given for making one piece will often serve for other things also. Thus, after the chisel, Lesson 1, has been made, there will be no difficulty in making any other punch or tool in steel.

It is too often forgotten that, just as a musician must

play a piece over and over again, until technical difficulties are completely mastered, if he wishes to express his own personality, so must the craftsman strive to reach a point where his work can be done with something like ease, abandon, and ecstasy.

If, therefore, we can find time to make two or more pieces of the same pattern at a time, we shall find great benefit from doing so. Our work will rid itself of all kinds of awkwardness and indecision. It will become broader, more urbane ; it will begin to show style.

The standards of accuracy and finish that the student should aim at need careful thought. Obviously, the smooth, hard smartness of ordinary factory-made work is impossible. Yet slovenly, untidy work, no matter how " artistic " it may be, is as bad, or worse. Here a study of the work of the past will help us enormously. We cannot compete with the machine, but we must remember that the human hand and eye can produce work, using the simplest tools, that is far beyond its reach.

Let us aim at the utmost accuracy, but let us take care that in achieving it our work does not become harsh and uninteresting.

LESSON 1

FILING A CHISEL OUT OF CAST STEEL ROD

Material.—Cast-steel rod, ⅜ in. square.

Tools.—A vice. A flat—" hand "—file, second cut, 8 in. or 10 in., preferably one that has had some wear: new files should never be used on steel if we wish them to last.[1] Two bits of scrap-metal for vice clams. A *hack-saw*. A smooth or superfine file of any shape. A pair of iron tongs. No. 1 emery cloth.

Cutting the steel.—This should be sawn through with a hack-saw to get the best results. Steel can be cut easily by filing a nick around at the desired point, when it will break at a sharp blow, if the piece be short, and with sharp pull if it be long; but this is likely to injure the quality of the tool: 2½ in. is the right length for our chisel.

Before we begin to use the file to shape our chisel we should read the section on files and filing in Chapter III, Section 3, carefully, so that we have a clear idea of what a file is and what it does.

The first thing to do with our length of steel is to file each end level and at right angles to every side of the bar. For this, of course, we use the large file.

The second is to put the steel in the vice, gripping it by two corners, so that the diagonals are horizontal

---

[1] A rough, three-square file, 12 in., is also good for making steel tools.

and vertical (Fig. 21). Then we file the angle away, making our square bar into an irregular octagon.

We now put the steel in the vice, protecting it from damage by the jaws by bending two bits of scrap-metal, shown in Fig. 13, Chapter III, Section 3, using them as clams. Fig. 22 shows the angle of the steel rod. Then we begin to file the corner away, first on one side, and then on the opposite side, until the shape shown by dotted lines in Fig. 23 A is reached. The plan of the end of the tool is then an oblong of $\frac{3}{8} \times \frac{3}{16}$ in. The centre of this oblong and the axis of the rod should coincide exactly. We have to file an equal amount from each side.

The next thing is to curve this tapering part of the bar or rod until the shape is like Fig. 23 B, except that the end is still an oblong $\frac{3}{8} \times \frac{1}{8}$ in. The whole must now be examined closely to detect inaccuracies.

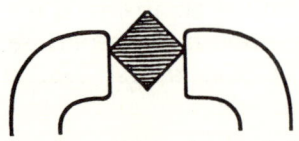

FIG. 21.—How the steel is gripped to file into an octagon.

We now change the large rough file for the smaller, smoother one. With this we file the whole lightly in the ordinary way to ensure the removal of deep scratches.

The deep scratches removed, we " draw file " the whole (see Chapter III, Section 3).

The chisel is now ready to receive its edge. This is got by filing bevels equally on both sides at an angle of about 25° to the axis until they meet in an edge, perfectly sharp, exactly parallel to the sides of the bar, and exactly on the axis (Fig. 23 B).

The edge and a space of about $\frac{1}{2}$ in. above it should now be polished on emery cloth. A convenient way is to lay the cloth on a flat surface and rub the chisel up and down upon it. Great care must be taken not to round or blunt any of our

SIX PRELIMINARY LESSONS

filed facets. All should be workmanlike and clean-cut in form.

We have come thus early on an instance of right methods of workmanship determining good form. It should always be our aim, in making tools, to make them as shapely and as pleasant to handle and to look on as we can. We shall in this way learn that fitness for purpose is essential to good form.

The chisel should now be hardened and tempered.

For this process see the section in Chapter III, Section 2.

We may find at our first attempt that we have made the chisel too hard or too soft. If too hard it may be tempered a little more. Remember that on bright steel, even when quite soft, the colours appear on heating just as they do when the steel is hard. A faint tinge of yellow, on a tool already tempered a little, will show that the process has gone far enough. The solid black at the lower end of Fig. 23 C shows the limit of the extreme hardness. Above this the temper should be much lower.

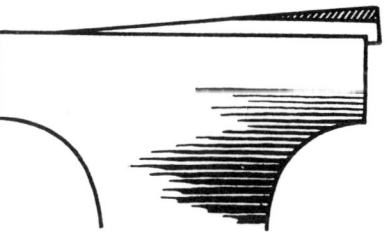

FIG. 22.—When tapering the chisel, put it in the vice at this angle.

All that now remains to be done is to " set " the edge of the chisel on an oil-stone. When the edge becomes so blunt that something that cuts more rapidly than the oil-stone is needed, we should grind it on a stone, if we have one. If not, a piece of coarse emery cloth, No. 2, blue back, glued on a board makes an efficient substitute.

The chisel we have made is very small, for the

reason that we need, for our next exercise, a tool that will cut quite thick metal cleanly and accurately, to an exact size. It will be held between the thumb and two

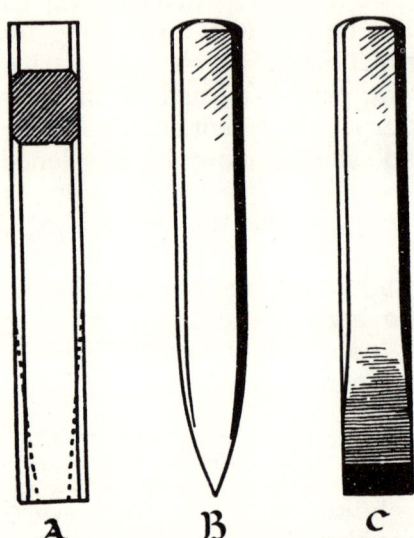

Fig. 23.—The chisel: A, in the making, B, side view, C, front view. Note the "striking" end of the chisel is rounded.

first fingers of the left hand. Its shortness makes it free from springiness, and we always get a firm, clean cut.

LESSON 2

CUTTING A PLATE, OR PLATES, AFTERWARDS TO BE MADE INTO ESCUTCHEONS, OR KEY-HOLE PLATES, FROM THICK BRASS [1]

Material.—Brass plate 6 in. wide, 14 S.W.G.
Tools.—Hammer, 10- or 12-oz. Chisel—made in Lesson 1. Steel rule. Dividers. Flat mallet. Flat die or anvil. Scrap-metal. Vice, clams, and files as Lesson 1.

What to make.—Nearly everyone can find a use for a well-made key-hole plate of pleasant shape.

This may be anything we please, so long as it is simple: a circle, a square, a hexagon, an octagon, a rectangle, a combination of rectangle and semicircles, and so on. The marking on, cutting out, and filing up of any one of these accurately provides an excellent exercise.

Cutting the rough blank.—The brass will probably be in pieces about 3 ft. long, and our little plate will be about $1\frac{1}{4}$ in. wide. Rule a line across at one end, at $1\frac{5}{16}$ in. from the edge. Place the brass on the anvil or the flat die with a piece of scrap-metal between it and the iron. If the brass be long we shall have to get someone to hold it. We then hold the edge of the chisel exactly on the line, and hit it smartly with the

[1] The figure given illustrates Lesson 6 as well as this Lesson.

hammer. We go on until we have a deep cut all across the brass. We then go on cutting more deeply until we feel that if the brass be bent across the cut it will break off, and give us a strip $6 \times 1\frac{1}{4}$ in. The actual breaking is conveniently done with a mallet. The cutting across transversely is a very simple matter. So long as we have a fairly stout piece of scrap-metal to keep the chisel edge from actual contact with the anvil, a flat iron plate, we may cut so deeply that the brass will break in our fingers.

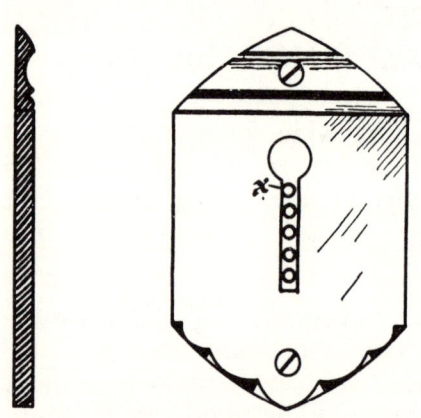

Fig. 24.—Side view. Key-hole plate, avoid drilling holes out of centre, as X.

As soon as the brass is chiselled roughly to shape it should be flattened with a few vigorous blows from a mallet. See Chapter III, Section 1, for preparation, and lessons 7 and 8 for use of this tool.

Marking on.—First see that the points of the dividers are sharp. They should be tested on the thumb nail. If they slip, they are too blunt, and should be rubbed on emery cloth, as one would a lead pencil, until when we rest the points on the nail we feel a distinct " bite." This is an infallible test for the edge of any metal-cutting tool.

Let us assume that we choose a plate as Fig. 24. We begin by filing one edge of our strip perfectly straight. This is not so easy as it seems. Files have a tendency to cut too much off the corners. We have to be careful that our wrists do not turn when the file reaches the ends of the strip. Vice clams must be used.

SIX PRELIMINARY LESSONS

With the dividers, set to the width we want, we strike a line parallel to the edge we have just trued. Then we file exactly up to this line, but without filing the line away. This is vastly important ; on it depends the accuracy of our work, not only here but always. We now have a parallel strip of brass.

Using the square we rule lines across at top and bottom of the rectangular part, and then strike the arcs from the extremities of these lines.[1] The chisel is used again, taking care not to come too close to the line. We then file up to the lines, and the first stage is completed.

The plate is examined for inaccuracies. The edges must everywhere be exactly at right angles to the faces. We should aim at keeping errors within $\frac{1}{100}$ in.

[1] With really sharp divider points we shall be able to have the centres of our arcs not more than $\frac{1}{64}$ in. from the edge.

LESSON 3

MAKING A "CENTRE" PUNCH

Material.—Cast-steel rod, round, ⅜ in. diameter.

Tools.—As before, with the addition of a hand vice, and a piece of wood, about 3 × 2 × 1 in. for a " filing block."

Cut the steel, as directed in Lesson 1, 3 in. long. File each end as drawn in Fig. 25; at first in the vice,

FIG. 25.—A centre punch: may be made octagonal if desired.

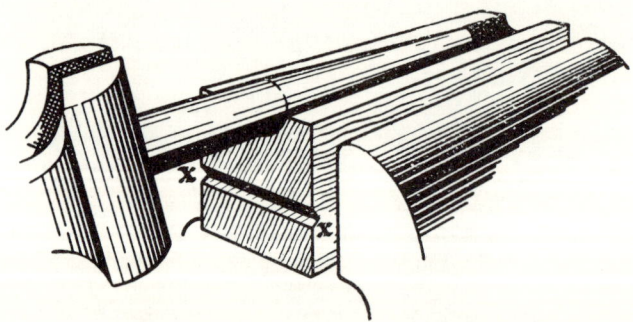

FIG. 26.—How a round rod is tapered.

and as an octagon. It may be left in that form, though the filing of the eight faces neatly and accurately will be difficult.

SIX PRELIMINARY LESSONS

Fig. 26 shows how to round the tapering ends. A groove is filed in the wood fastened in the vice. The steel, screwed firmly in the hand vice (clams are needed), is placed in the groove and turned slowly backwards and for.....ds with the left hand. We shall then find we can file it quite easily with the right hand only. At the end of this stage the small end is flat ; in plan a $\frac{1}{8}$-in. circle.

The point, as nearly as possible an angle of 90°, is filed by resting the end of the punch in the groove, turning it slowly round, and filing across at the correct angle.

Harden and temper as the chisel, but a little nearer a brown colour.

LESSON 4

MAKING A SCRIBER

Material.—Cast-steel rod, $\frac{3}{16}$ in. square.
Tools.—As before.

Cut a 6-in. length of the steel. File it till its section is a regular octagon. Taper it on each face till the ends are octagons of $\frac{1}{16}$ in. Draw file and emery cloth the two ends. File a point on one end as Fig. 27, and a similar point on the other, but much more obtuse. Harden and temper, the tips only, to full brown.[1] If desired this may be made from round steel in the manner of the centre punch.

FIG. 27.—Scriber. Try to get the eight faces shapely, of even taper.

The scriber is used for setting out, on the actual metal, the form or shape of what we want to make. The acute end is used for ruling lines. The blunt end for marking the position of drill holes. These are afterwards deepened by the centre punch.

It is not absolutely necessary to make a scriber at this stage. We may use a point of the dividers instead. It is, however, a most useful tool to have, and its making gives excellent practice.

---

[1] When hardening long thin things be careful to plunge vertically. This lessens the tendency to warp and twist.

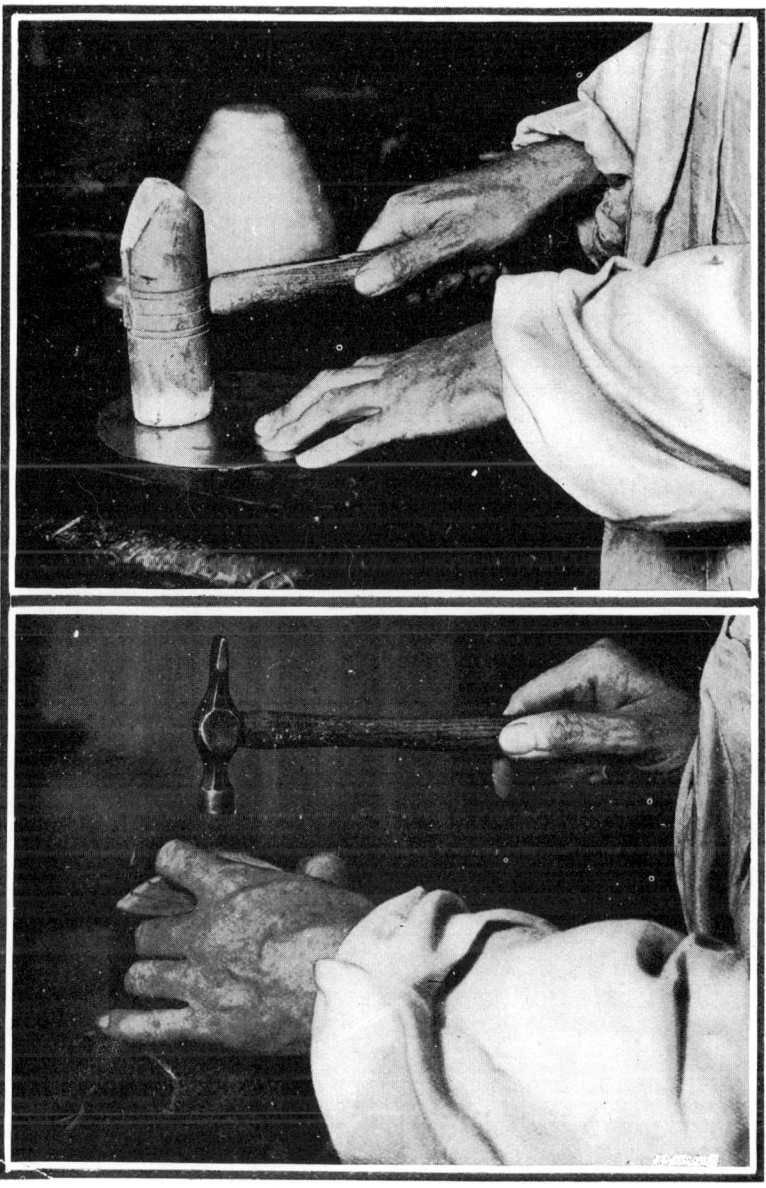

Above: Fig. 30.—Flattening metal with a mallet on the flat die. (See footnote on page 90.)

Below: Fig. 31.—Planishing a shallow tray. (See footnote on page 93.)

LESSON 5

DRILL MAKING (SPEAR OR DIAMOND POINT)

Material.—" Silver " steel rods, $\frac{1}{8}$ in. and $\frac{5}{32}$ in. diameter. The name is that given to fine quality steel rods finished bright, usually 12 in. long. There is, of course, no silver in the composition of the steel. The name comes from its colour.

Tools.—As before. *Oil* for hardening.

We will make the large drill, to bore a hole of $\frac{11}{64}$ in. diameter, first. Cut a length of steel 2 in. or so, and file the ends flat. Grip it in the hand vice so that rather more than half of it projects. Put the filing block (Lesson 3, Fig. 26) in the vice, with the end of the grain uppermost, and the 1-in. measurement parallel with the jaws. In the wood file a groove, about $\frac{3}{16}$ in. wide and $\frac{3}{32}$ in. deep. The groove is, of course, 1 in. long. (See Lesson 3, Fig. 26.)

Hold the steel in this groove, and with the cutting edge of a flat file for roughing, and for finishing the rounded part of a half-round, file it to the shape of 1. Fig. 28.

Then, holding the knob on the edge of the anvil or flat die, with the large end, or " shank," pointing away from the edge, strike it smartly with the hammer, and spread it out as 2 : 2 A shows a side view.

With practice a drill can be held in the fingers for flattening. At first it is as well to use the hand vice.

The axis of the drill should make an angle of about 15° with the face of the anvil.

The flattened end is now filed, as shown at 3 and 3 A. The two right-hand angles are bevelled, one on each side; this gives the two cutting edges. Finally, the extreme tip is made a little thinner (note the end and side view of 4), and the sides of the drill are filed

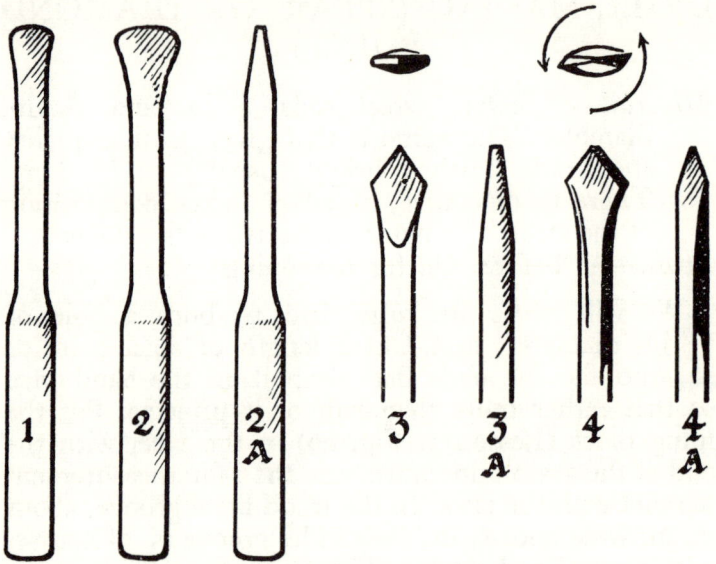

FIG. 28.—Stages in making a " spear-point " drill.

back (see 4 A) so as to give more clearance, or space for the cuttings to come away.

If we could see the tip of a drill as it cuts its way through the metal we should see it revolving in a counter-clock-wise direction.

The drill is now hardened, right up to the shank, in oil, not water, to make it tough, and tempered to a purple, all except the extreme tip, which should be yellow.

It is not quite an easy matter to harden and temper drills. The thinner part of the stem, as well as the cutting edge, has to be hardened to prevent bending, yet it has to be so elastic that it will stand much strain; and then the end itself has to be sufficiently hard to keep the edges sharp.

After hardening and tempering, the edges, shaded in end view of 4, are sharpened on an oil-stone.

The small drill, to bore holes of $\frac{5}{64}$ in. or $\frac{3}{32}$ in., should be made in exactly the same way. For smaller drills still, a four-jaw split-pin vice is handier than a hand vice.

We must accustom ourselves from the first to make drills to exact sizes. For this, a wire gauge is most convenient. All we have to do, after we have made our drill (we should always keep it a shade on the large side in the first stages) is to file the sides and lower parts of the cutting edges away until the drill will just pass the slot of the size we want. If we have no gauge we must file a slot in a bit of metal. It is impossible to determine the size of a drill by measurement with a rule to any degree of accuracy.

If we wish to reduce the size of a drill after it has been hardened and tempered, we can grind it with emery cloth or on an oil-stone.

A good drill should (*a*) cut quickly; (*b*) centre well, that is, bore a perfectly round hole exactly in the position marked by the centre punch; (*c*) have good clearance—a drill should not need constant withdrawal to remove cuttings. The real test comes when we try to drill a hole through metal $\frac{1}{4}$ in. or more thick.

Some metals will drill without oil, but some will not. It is always safer to assume that oil will be needed. This will prevent breakage.

If a drill should break in metal, in such a way that we cannot pull it out, the only thing to be done is to heat the whole piece of work to redness, so as to soften the broken piece of drill. It is then possible to bore a hole from the other side until the new drill meets the broken piece, when it can be driven out with a punch.

If it should be thought that drill making will take up too much time, we can buy " twist " drills of any size, though below $\frac{1}{16}$ in. they are not suitable for hand-drill stocks. As supplied they are too long for hand stocks, and the shank should be cut off. It is difficult to sharpen twist drills without a special appliance.

See Chapter III, Section 4, for further notes on drilling.

LESSON 6

COMPLETING THE ESCUTCHEON BEGUN IN LESSON 2:

(Refer to figure in that lesson.)
Material.—Already provided.
Tools.—As before : the centre punch, scriber, drills, drill stock, and needle files, three-square, double half-round, flat, in addition.

Begin by marking a line exactly down the centre of the plate. Its surface is still untouched, although the edges have been filed to shape. Upon this line punch the centres of the screw holes and the large hole at top of the slot. Then mark the centres of a series of holes down the length of the slot. (See figure, Lesson 2).

Test the drills on a bit of scrap-metal. In fact, it will be as well for anyone who has never used a drill to drill a number of trial holes before starting on the plate.

The holding of the metal is not quite easy. If we put it in the vice we may find we cannot do what we want. The chuck of the drill stock may come against the vice jaws, or something else may turn up, and be inconvenient.

On the other hand, if we lay the plate on the bench, putting a bit of wood to prevent damage to the bench top, we shall find that just as the drill is coming through it will stick and make the plate spin round. If help is available, it can be held by another hand. If not, the best thing is to cut a groove in a bit of wood ;

or to nail two strips on it just far enough apart to allow the plate to drop between them.

Some care is needed in marking and drilling the holes down the slot. Their centres must come exactly on the axis of the plate, and the holes must be just far enough apart to avoid the drill breaking through into its neighbours.

The metal between the holes can now be filed away with the flat needle file. Care should be taken that the slot is central on the plate, and that its centre, and the centre of the hole for the pipe of the key, are on the axis, after the filing is done. It is fatally easy to file a little more on one side than on the other.

Figure 24, Lesson 2, shows two different treatments for the ends. The lower one is the easier. This is done with a three-square needle file. The plate is held on the peg, or a bit of wood held in the vice. (See Chapter III, Section 3, Fig. 14.[1])

In starting the bevelling, after it has been marked on carefully, we shall find a guide for the first few strokes of the file is needed. The professional worker would use his thumb, which, with constant use, becomes covered with thick hard skin. If we cannot do this we must use a bit of thin wood or a bit of scrap-metal held tightly on the escutcheon for this guidance.

It should be noted that the bevelling does not extend to the back of the plate. The filing would be easier if it did, but a clear outline, to allow no lodgment for dirt, is a good point in an escutcheon.

This simple bit of filing is a good introduction to the

---

[1] This photograph shows work of a quite different nature being done. The key-hole plate would be held at an angle of about 40° with the vertical. It would be gripped between the thumb and forefinger. The left hand would, of course, be below the peg. It will often be found the greatest help to allow the file to ride on the peg and to bring the work to it, rather than to bring the file to the work.

SIX PRELIMINARY LESSONS

use of a file in modelled, as distinct from flat, filing. We shall find the secret of getting clean even curves lies in the right correlation between the backward and forward strokes of the file and the turning movement given to it by the wrist.

The moulding of the upper end in Fig. 24 is shown on the section, drawn on the left. To begin it take a piece of scrap-metal long enough to go all across the plate, file one end perfectly straight, and cramp it on to the plate with the hand vice so that the straight edge lies across in a straight line joining the ends of the centre rectangle. Then, with the angle of a three-square file, its face next the brass strip being vertical, a notch is filed all across the plate. The other notch is filed in the same way. Then the strip is moved still farther out, and the extreme point is thinned down with a curved surface. The hollow between this rounded moulding and the outer notch is made with the back of a half-round file, using a double half-round needle file for finishing. The round moulding between the two notches can be got by wrist action making the three-square file turn over as it moves to and fro.

When we have filed the ends of the plate as finely as we can (meaning fineness of contour rather than of surface), we file the whole surface over lightly, and in constantly changing directions, to remove any deep scratches or other blemishes. Then we emery cloth the whole. For the flat surface use an emery stick—the oblong strip of wood wrapped round with emery cloth. For the curved surfaces we use bits of the same emery cloth wrapped around the files. Remember to emery cloth the edges of the plate.

Finally, the plate can be polished with pumice and oil ; either with a brush, hand, a lathe, or a piece of wood anointed with the paste. The lustre can be raised with metal-polish.

The plate has purposely been drawn too wide so that there shall be no temptation to copy it. Experiments in the cutting out of shapes in paper should be tried, varying the proportions of height and width, of relation between straight and curved outline, and so on. By simple means of this kind one trains one's knowledge and taste. Good design, it should always be remembered, does not necessarily mean elaboration or strangeness. It is like fine literature, where every word adds to the effect of the whole, and is charged with an intensity of meaning.

The exercise has been chosen because it is one that brings out clearly the essential quality of filed brasswork. It would look wrong if made in silver.

The light falling on the moulded surface of the brass gives differences of light, shade, and colour. By skilful choice of hollows, of rounded surfaces, of sharp edges, alone and in combination, we get a quality akin to colour. Like colours, these qualities can be harmonised or contrasted, and like colours be made to express our deepest thoughts and feelings.

LESSON 7

A SIMPLE DISH OR TRAY

This lesson introduces the student to the use of: The hammer.—Blow-pipe for soldering—hard or soft—Polishing materials, "Water of Ayr" stone, etc.

Materials.—Copper, brass, or gilding metal sheet, 5 in. × 5 in. × 22 S.W.G. Brass or gilding metal plate $6\frac{1}{2}$ in. × 5 in. × 14 S.W.G. Brass or gilding metal strip (cut from sheet) $6\frac{1}{2}$ in. × $\frac{5}{16}$ in. × 16 S.W.G. Solder—hard and easy silver, or soft solder. Flux. Borax or killed spirit.

Tools.—As before, with the addition of a hammer 4 oz. Stake, Fig. 6, Chapter II. Mandrel, $1\frac{1}{2}$ in. to 3 in. diameter, any size that will fit the ring foot. Shears, pliers 8 in. straight. Scraper, Fig. 37. "Water of Ayr" stone. Sand-bag or wood-block. Hearth and blow-pipe, or Bunsen-burner. Pickle vat. Cotter-pins. Binding wire. Sawdust or towel.

This exercise is intended to give the beginner, who hitherto has been working within very rigid limits, a wider scope.

Fig. 29 shows a tray in plan and elevation. It may be made large, say $7\frac{1}{2}$ in. over all, when we may have it silver-plated for use as a sweet dish; or on a smaller scale, when it will serve for a pin- or ash-tray. It must be understood that the following method is intended for the absolute beginner.

If the student has had any previous experience in

90 A FIRST BOOK OF METAL-WORK

metal-work he may adopt any method he pleases in making the rim of the tray. He may saw pierce instead of chipping it ; or he may make it out of oblong wire, adding pieces of plate for the handles. It is, however, the writer's opinion that the method given is the best for the very young student to attempt.

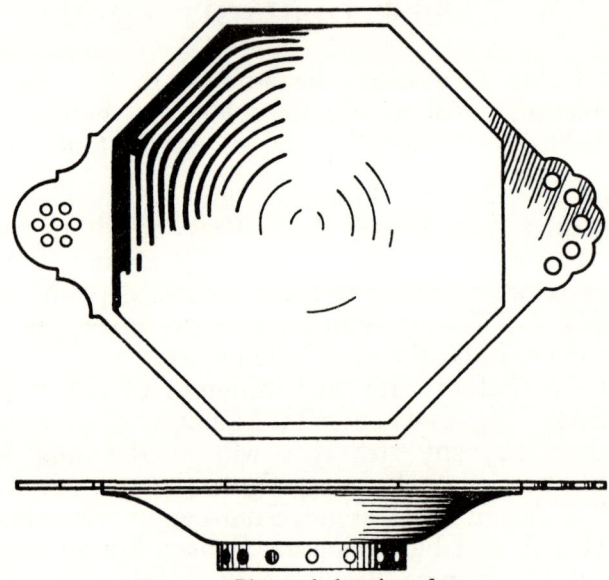

FIG. 29.—Plan and elevation of tray.

The first thing is to make the rim. Take the plate of brass (it is assumed that we shall use that metal throughout, though it would look equally well in copper, with a brass rim and foot, or in gilding metal throughout), flatten with the mallet (Fig. 30[1]), and upon it mark out with the greatest care and accuracy the inner

[1] Note in the photograph the way the handle, or stail, is gripped. The thumb is extended and pressed lightly against it, the blow is struck from the wrist only. The upper and forearms are pressed against the body and remain still. (Facing page 80.)

A SIMPLE DISH OR TRAY

octagon (Fig. 29). Then a little way within each corner drill a hole with the larger drill we have made, and with the chisel cut a line joining them; we shall probably have to go round twice, when the centre piece will fall out, or come out with only a little tapping and bending.

We now have an octagonal hole in the plate, which we enlarge and true up with the file until it is exactly the size we need. Do not forget to use vice clams. Take care not to file the scribed line away. With the dividers mark the outer lines, parallel to edge on six of the sides. The lugs or handles on the other sides should be marked now, also with the greatest care and accuracy. We shall of course make some change from the drawing. Even in this simple piece we shall find ample scope for using our own powers of design. The width of the rim may be altered. It need not be rigidly straight-lined. The handles can be altered in size and shape to any extent we please, and if we can use hammer and punch, we shall find it quite a good subject for decoration.

The outer edge is now cut out with drill (use this very freely, so that distortion may be avoided) and chisel. Straighten out, by tapping with the mallet and smaller hammer, on the flat die, any parts that may have got bent. Give it a preliminary polish with emery cloth.

We are now ready for the tray. Shear an octagon $4\frac{7}{8}$ in. diameter from the 22 S.W.G. sheet.[1] Take the sand-bag, if we have it; if not, we may use a piece of deal 2 in. or 3 in. square; put in the vice with its end grain uppermost, and with a gouge take out a hollow about $\frac{1}{2}$ in. or $\frac{3}{4}$ in. deep in the centre, according to the size of the wood.

On the sand-bag, or the wood, with the ball pane of our larger hammer (take care that this is as clean,

[1] Take the same care in filing as in shearing to ensure accuracy. Cut up to the line, but do not cut it away.

bright, and smooth as emery cloth will make it) beat the octagon into a shallow saucer shape (see Fig. 40, facing page 96). At this stage it should be a little deeper than the finished piece is to be.

We are now ready for the stake (Fig. 6, Chapter II). If we have only the rough malleable casting we must file it up. Begin with a rough file, a 12-in. or 14-in. " Sheffield " three-square rough is excellent for the purpose. Then use a smooth file, stroking it in every direction. Finally, finish with emery cloth. A sheet of No. 2 or 3 blue-back emery cloth tacked on a piece of 1-in. board $2\frac{1}{2}$ in. or 3 in. wide and 13 in. or 14 in. long is excellent for this. Finish with F.F., used in the same way.

As the inner side is in this piece more important than the outside, the surface of the stake is all important. Upon its smoothness the texture of the tray will depend.

We are now ready for " planishing "[1] the tray. If we have a hearth and pickle ready we should anneal the octagon, and after it has cooled put it in the pickle until the oxide is dissolved (see note on annealing and pickling, Chapter III, Section 2). If we have no hearth and no pickle we can manage without annealing, but this is not good practice. We could anneal the brass by holding it in a Bunsen-flame, and then clean it with a stiff brush, using pumice powder and water, a rather lengthy business.

The first thing to do is to mark with pencil compasses a 1-in. circle in the centre of the outer, or convex, side; other circles, increasing in radius by $\frac{1}{2}$ in., should then be drawn to the edges of the octagon. Then give it an even, but vigorous, malleting until it is reasonably smooth.

Before we begin the actual hammering with the

---

[1] " Planishing," as its name indicates, is the making of metal smooth and even by hammering it on a bright stake, or head, with a bright smooth hammer.

A SIMPLE DISH OR TRAY

4-oz. hammer, we shall do well to study the photograph, Fig. 31,[1] showing the proper grip; and to read the notes in Chapter III, Section 1, and to practise on bits of scrap-metal to make ourselves familiar with the actual use of the hammer in planishing.

As soon as we have gained some measure of confidence, we can begin on the tray itself. Place it on the stake, and hold it in such a way that when the hammer falls we shall feel it fall on something solid. Then go evenly over the centre circle, until every part has been made smooth (planished) by contact with the hammer on one side and the smooth bright stake on the other.

Now place the tray so that when it is revolved the next ring marked on the bottom will pass over the centre of the stake. The tray is now turned round slowly, and as it moves the hammer rises and falls regularly and planishes this ring. We shall find it necessary to move the point at which we aim the hammer blow a little in and out, so that the whole width of the ½-in. wide circular space is covered with hammer blows. Sometimes we may have to move the work we are planishing, instead of moving the point of the hammer's contact. Experience and practice will enable us to decide which is the better course.

It may seem a rather difficult matter to tell the exact spot on the outer surface of a bowl, etc., where the stake is in close contact underneath. We shall find soon that we depend as much on feel and sound as we do on sight. Whenever we fail to find this spot we may press the bowl tightly on to the stake with the face of the hammer, and it will be revealed at once.

---

[1] Note the way the hammer is gripped, and how the metal is held: the thumb and forefinger are extended, the metal is pressed on to the head, or stake, with their tips; the hammer falls between them. This method ensures contact between tray and stake. It is not always possible to employ it, but it is the easiest and best for many things. (Facing page 80.)

Planishing demands a combination of caution and courage.

Each ring in its turn is planished. Then we go over the piece again, quite lightly; this time the lines of hammer blows will move radially instead of concentrically. This will make the whole perfectly smooth and even in contour.

As soon as we have satisfied ourselves that the tray

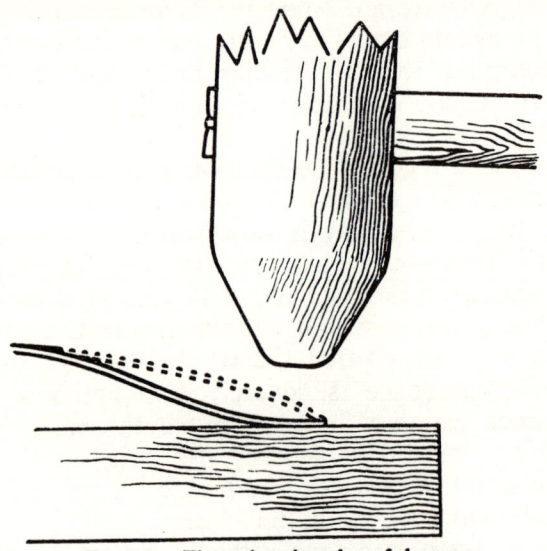

FIG. 32.—Flattening the edge of the tray.

is as fine in form and texture as we can make it, we anneal it again and clean it, by pickle or by scouring.

We have now to flatten the edge of the tray so that the rim will lie on it and be in contact on both its inner and outer edges (see Fig. 32).

We need a mallet, sawn and filed as Fig. 32. Do not forget the need for filing it quite smooth, and be careful to get rid of all traces of wood-dust.

Draw an octagon on the convex side of the tray.

A SIMPLE DISH OR TRAY

This should be, in diameter, $\frac{1}{2}$ in. less than the opening in the rim, so as to show a space of $\frac{1}{4}$ in. all round.

The tray is now held on the flat die, and each of the eight sides is, in turn, flattened down on to the iron with the blunt-pointed end of the mallet. The handle of the mallet is, of course, at right angles to each side of the octagon as its turn comes (Fig. 32). It will be found that the mallet will in no way damage the hammered surface. We must be careful to make the iron die as smooth and bright as we can. If we find the rim of the tray refuses to lie down evenly—it may tend to spring up—we should put a piece of card between the iron and the tray, and again strike along the edges with the mallet. It may even need annealing again.

If we have planished and shaped our tray carefully, in the simple, natural way described, we shall inevitably have made something pleasant to look upon.

If we are working in a class where numbers of this same thing are being made together, we shall see surprising differences between them. Some will show greater sensitiveness to subtle qualities of form and texture than will others. One of the vital things about hand-work is that it is like handwriting: it does express its author's personality.

Careful craftsmanship will not fail to produce an interesting shape. The contact of tool with material, it cannot too often be pointed out, will ensure rightness of form of itself.

Next comes the making of the ring foot on which the tray stands. Assuming that we have a hearth and blow-pipe we will hard solder it. Cut the strip from the 16 S.W.G. brass, $3\frac{1}{7}$ times the diameter in length, file it exactly parallel, the ends exactly at right angles (these should be done with a rough file), bend it up

96 A FIRST BOOK OF METAL-WORK

Fig. 33.—The ring wired for soldering.

into a ring, and secure in position with binding wire: 20 S.W.G. is a good thickness (Fig. 33).

Mix some powdered borax with water, and paint, with the brush, a little of the cream all round the seam, making sure that it goes right through the joining place. Place the ring on the hearth. Play the blow-pipe flame upon it, at first without any blast, then with a gentle blast, until the borax ceases to bubble. The blow-pipe is held in the left hand with its nozzle pointing downwards, at an angle, normally, of 45°.

When we first apply the flame to our work it should be about 8 in. long for small work, to 12 in. or 14 in. for large. When we need to shorten and intensify the flame, these distances are reduced, sometimes even halved.

Have in readiness a few snips—" panels "—of solder about $\frac{3}{16} \times \frac{1}{16}$ in. of 25 S.W.G. or 8 M.G. thickness. Take one or two up in the corn-tongs or tweezers, dip in the borax cream, and place on the seam inside the ring. Fig. 34 shows positions, and how the ring is leant against a bit of brick or coke.

Again apply the flame as before, taking care that when the blast is put on the flame first plays on the opposite side of the ring to the seam. This has the effect, through the expansion of the

Fig. 34.—The ring, charged with solder in position for soldering.

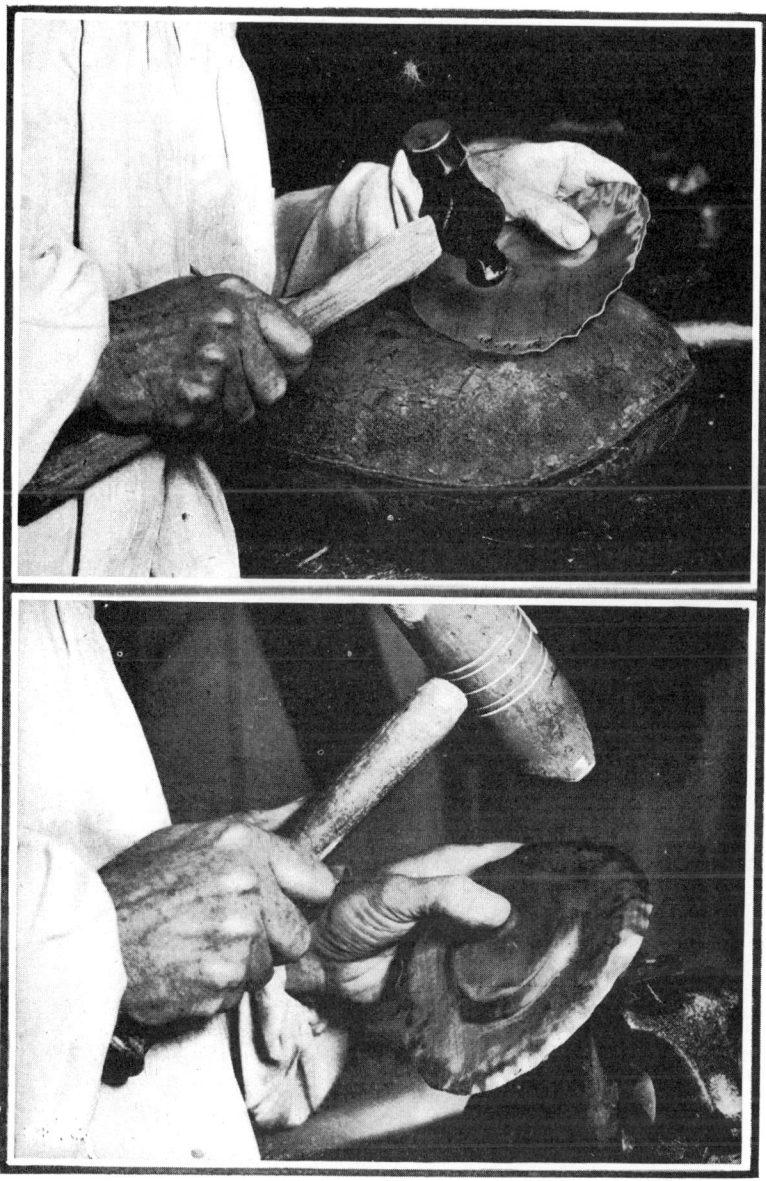

Above: FIG. 40. "Bellying" or "doming" or "turning up" the edge of the blank in preparation for raising. (See footnote, page 106.)

Below: FIG. 42.—The "first course." Beginning a raising. If the raising were transparent we should see that the forefinger of the left hand touches the head. This is a great help in turning the raising truly. (Compare Fig. 43.)

metal, of forcing the ends of the strip forming the ring closer together. A few experiments with rings of scrap-metal will be valuable in helping us to understand how the metal behaves when expanding.

At our first attempts it is probable that the panels of solder will fly off. The behaviour of borax under heat makes difficulties. The more slowly we apply the heat the less trouble there will be.[1]

When we find we can go on heating without disturbing the solder, we increase flame and blast, making the whole ring hot. The one thing we have to avoid is making one end of the strip very hot, while the other remains, by comparison, cool. Here again experiment will show us that we may make one end of a strip, bent into a ring, red-hot, while the other remains comparatively cold and black. Heat is not conducted, to a great degree, across the actual join. When we see the metal on both sides of the seam getting red-hot, we reduce the flame, increase the blast, and move the flame rapidly to and fro over the seam, until we see the solder flush and rush in a glistening stream along the join.

Allow the ring to cool a little before quenching (sudden cooling is not always safe). Remove the binding wire. If we cannot get it to move with pliers we must file it off. When one is experienced this trouble lessens, and in stubborn cases one can heat the soldered thing again and pull the binding wire off while hot. Do not try this yet. When clear of iron put the ring in the pickle.

Iron is never put into sulphuric acid pickle. Undesirable chemical action takes place. For our present purpose we need a hook of sheet metal, or wire, on which we can hang our ring.

---

[1] Borax—biborate of sodium—contains much water. Until this is driven off, heat will make it swell and bubble violently.

The ring must be left in the pickle until all traces of the borax, which will have fused into a hard glassy substance, have been dissolved away. Then it is taken out and swilled in water, running if possible, until no trace of acid is left. Put it back on the hearth. Play the flame on it for a moment, and wipe it dry on rag, or rough towel.

File the solder away, taking care that as soon as the white solder has been removed the filing stops. This applies to the outside particularly. When we have to put the solder on from the outside we have to be extremely careful. Our aim is to leave but the thinnest of white lines showing.

We may now round the ring foot on the mandrel, first with the mallet and then with the hammer. Be careful to strike exactly in the middle of the strip forming the ring, if this is not done first we shall find the edge will stretch, and the sides of the ring go out of the vertical. If our ring were of thinner metal we should need to be even more careful. Aim at giving a pleasant smooth texture to the ring with the flat hammer.

If we have no large tapering mandrel, we may make shift with quite a small straight one, by holding the ring at an angle to its axis. A line traced on a cylindrical surface at an angle of some degrees, 45° or more, is a very much flatter curve than a piece of the circumference. By taking advantage of this we can make one stake serve a number of purposes.

The ring being true, we rub one edge level on a piece of emery cloth laid on the flat die. From this edge we find out if the other one is parallel. If not we file it until it is so, giving it finally a rub on the emery.

If we decide that this ring is too bald and uninteresting, we may enliven it in one of these two ways : we may drill a series of holes as drawn, or we may file it

A SIMPLE DISH OR TRAY

into a series of vertical mouldings, in the manner suggested for one end of the escutcheon in Lesson 6. The simplest form of this would be a series of grooves, made with a half-round needle file.

We may now solder the rim on to the tray. Do not forget to brighten the surfaces to be joined, with scraper or emery cloth. Fig. 35 shows two ways of securing them together for this. The left-hand X shows binding wire [1] folded or bent under and over in

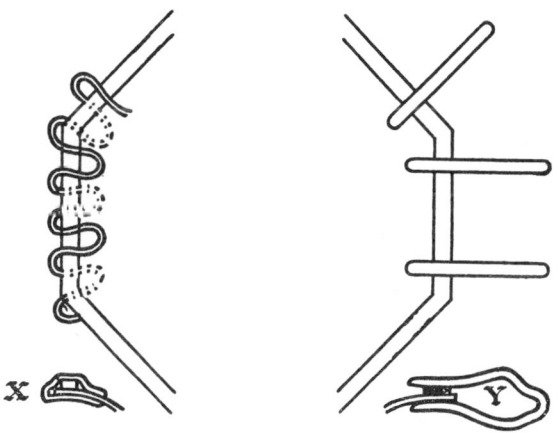

Fig. 35.—Two methods of securing the rim to the tray for soldering.

loops. These loops are afterwards tightened by holding the wired tray on the flat die and pushing the wire firmly with some hard instrument, such as the end of a file, into the angles between rim and tray. This holds the rim quite firmly in position. Before this bending is done the rim is sufficiently loose for us to adjust its position with great nicety.

The right-hand Y shows the use of cotter-pins. These are first opened out and bent into a similar

[1] 20 S.W.G. is a normal gauge.

shape to that shown. Sometimes it may be necessary to anneal them beforehand. Trade workers use short lengths of iron wire flattened at both ends, and bent into a similar shape. When only a few of these " cramps " are clipped on, the final adjustment can be made with ease. The cramping could be done with eight cramps only, but sixteen would be far better for a beginner.

The rim being cramped on the tray (take care to scrape the under side of the rim bright and to emery cloth the upper side of the tray so as to ensure the contact of two clean metallic surfaces), the join between rim and tray is boraxed, dried off, panels of solder [1] are put in position, and the whole heated until the solder flushes. The panels of solder are, of course, put in the outer angle between rim and tray. (The rule in soldering is always to apply it from the side or position from whence the surplus may most easily be removed.) Gentle heating at first, followed by a gradual increase of temperature, and a final flushing by a smaller, fiercer flame in rapid motion, directed along the join, should give us a sound result. The rapid motion of the flame enables us to use safely a heat that would melt brass if allowed to be directed on one spot continuously.

Jobs such as this are most conveniently done on a revolving hearth. If we haven't one we shall have to move our blow-pipe over a wider area. Even so, on work of this kind we shall often have to turn our work around with tongs, so that the flame strikes the work from all sides.

Some thought is called for in placing the work on the hearth. The tray itself is of comparatively thin, and the rim of thick metal. Thin metal, of course, gets hot before thick, and solder will always flow to the

---

[1] About four $\frac{3}{16} \times \frac{1}{16}$ in. of the thick " easy " solder will be needed on each of the eight sides.

hottest point. The tendency, therefore, will be for the solder to spread over the tray. This will be unsightly, and the solder will be difficult to remove.

What we have to do is to arrange our bits of coke, or our wire gauze, or our pad, wig, or boss of used binding wire (this should be kept until a circular pad of tangled wire, say 8 in. diameter and $\frac{1}{2}$ in. thick, can be made, Fig. 51) in such a way that, while they support the work with the least danger of getting out of shape (remember that when metals are intensely hot they are extremely soft), we can apply the heat so that the thick parts of our work get hot quickly.

If, in this present case, we have a flat brick, it might seem as if the best thing to do would be to lay our tray, rim downwards, in contact with the flat surface. Were we to do so, we should find it difficult to get the thick rim hot enough. It would be impossible to use panels of solder in this upside down position.

We must have a pair of large tweezers—" corn tongs "—handy, or a pair of light iron tongs of the ordinary jointed kind at hand so that if the tray and rim show any sign of coming away from each other they may be squeezed gently together while the solder is still fused.

Next we fit the ring foot on to the tray. This may be done before cleaning the tray. Any oxide on the bottom can be scoured off with emery cloth before soldering. The inner corner of the ring should be filed off at an angle to make a better fit. Mark a circle on the tray, with dividers, of such a size as to be just visible inside the ring. Place it in position, and see if it fits closely all around. If it does not, notice the points of contact. Lower these with a smooth file until even contact is obtained all round. Experience alone will teach us the amount of accuracy needed, but speaking roughly we may say that solder will fill gaps of $\frac{1}{100}$ in. quite easily.

The fitting accomplished, wire the foot in position. Figure 51 in Lesson 8 shows the method. The loops are twisted (always turn to the right to tighten) to get the necessary pull. Borax, charge[1] with about ten or twelve panels of the easy solder, and fire. It will be well to put a piece of binding wire around the foot while this is done, so that there is no danger of our melting the soldered seam, and thus making it gape open.

The tray should now be examined carefully. If any gaps in the soldering appear, apply more, and fire again.

This done, pickle perfectly clean, swill, scour, and dry. Shear away, as closely as possible without damaging the rim, the projecting edge of the tray (Fig. 36) and file up close.

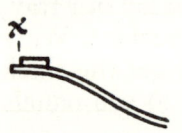

FIG. 36.—Section of rim of tray. The projection x, beyond, is sheared and filed away.

Remove any surplus solder from around the ring foot with a file. Emery cloth the file marks away, and the whole is ready for polishing, unless we find there are still some tiny crevices remaining that need to be filled up with solder. If there are we must be careful not to fire any harder than is needed to fill the gap; otherwise we may find we shall fill up one crevice only to find others have opened.

Soft soldering.—If by any chance we have no blow-pipe and our only heating appliance is a Bunsen-burner or a painter's blow-lamp, we may make quite a good job of the tray with soft solder.

Even with the substitutes mentioned above, it would be possible, even easy, to silver solder the strip to make it into a ring foot. With the Bunsen-burner we should

---

[1] When we place panels of solder on a piece of work preparatory to soldering we speak of "charging."

A SIMPLE DISH OR TRAY

have to hold the ring in the flame. It would be possible to manage without soldering the seam of the ring at all until it is actually put on the bottom of the tray. This we should do merely by keeping the ring of iron binding wire around it until the very last.

Except that we need a different flux and much less intense heat, the exact methods given for hard solder should be followed.

The soft soldering completed, the whole will need to be washed in hot water with soap powder to ensure the removal of all trace of acid.

When we clean off the surplus solder, however, we shall need to scrape it off with a scraper (Fig. 37). If possible, avoid using a file on soft solder; it clogs the teeth badly, and spoils them quickly.

Fig. 37.—A scraper. The hook end is pulled towards the worker. The pointed end is triangular in section.

The scraper must be kept very sharp by constantly rubbing the small face on the oil-stone. Keep this face as flat as possible.

Any traces of soft solder that may be left after scraper and emery cloth have done their work will yield to the vigorous brushing with pumice and oil that we shall give to our tray. If we have used hard solder we shall brush our work in exactly the same way; but we must not expect the pumice and oil to remove any appreciable amount of hard solder. File, emery cloth, and "Water of Ayr" stone are needed to take all the white patches clean away.

The final finish to the tray may be given by brushing with Tripoli or rotten-stone and oil. If there should be any patches of uneven colour, we may "dip" the tray in diluted nitric acid until it becomes an even yellow. This will dull the surface slightly, and necessitate refinishing.

If we want a very bright finish, we can use any good

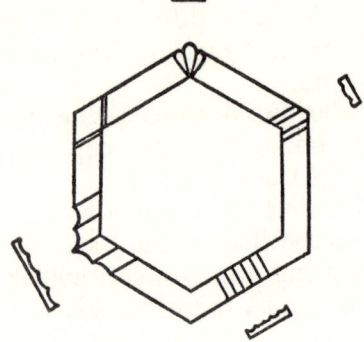

Fig. 38.—Smaller trays of similar construction make pleasant pieces.

metal-polish, taking care to wash the last traces away with hot water and soap.

Small trays, say 3 in. diameter, made in a similar way with broad rims, say ⅜ in., would make excellent ash-trays. Fig. 38 shows how these rims might be treated.

LESSON 8

RAISING, HAMMERING, AND MOUNTING A BOWL

THIS lesson contains in itself an account of almost all the simpler methods used, by the silversmith and metal-worker, in fashioning vessels out of sheet metal by the use of mallets and hammers. It deals, at some length, with soldering.

Material.—A circle of any malleable metal, of the desired diameter, about 21 S.W.G. Half-round wire, $\frac{1}{8}$ in. across flat side. Oblong wire $\frac{1}{4}$ in. wide × $\frac{5}{64}$ in. thick. Strip, $\frac{5}{8}$ in. or $\frac{3}{4}$ in. wide (according to size of bowl), cut from sheet 16 S.W.G. Brass, wire or grain, for soldering seams of wires, if gilding metal is used.

Tools.—As before, with the addition of crank and stakes (Figs. 3, 4, 5, 6,[1] Chapter II). Neck hammer and large mandrel. Scribing block.

The methods given are applicable to the fashioning of bowls of any shape or size. The foot may be omitted, if desired, but the planishing of a flat base is difficult. The student may have a perfectly free hand; but he will be wise to choose a very simple shape to begin with.

We will begin with a bowl roughly hemispherical (Fig. 39). Cut a disc of metal 23 S.W.G. if under 6 in., and 21 S.W.G. if over that size. Take care to shear exactly up to the circle scribed with the dividers. Then with a smooth file, round the edge of the disc slightly:

[1] A "mushroom" head, as Fig. 6, but more rounded, will be all that is needed for a hemispherical bowl.

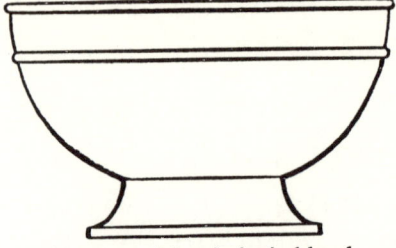

FIG. 39.—A hemispherical bowl.

this is done in the interests of one's fingers. A raw sheared edge will give a nasty cut. Scour both sides of the disc clean with a bit of wet rag dipped in powdered pumice. This will reveal any blemishes there may be. If we find the metal has patches where the surface is flaky reject the disc and cut another. " Spilly " metal, rolled from faulty ingots, is useless : it tends to split or laminate. Metal deeply scratched or bruised should also be rejected.

To begin actual raising : see that the centre, on what is to be the outer side, is clearly marked by pushing the point of a leg of the dividers firmly into the metal. Then, holding the disc on a hollow in a wooden block, or on a sand-bag, beat it from the inner side with the ball pane of the hammer (Fig. 40[1]) until its section is like Fig. 41. This is done to stiffen the disc. Anneal it and pickle clean. Now take a pair of pencil compasses and draw a concentric circle on the outer convex side of the disc, about two-fifths of the disc's diameter.

Put a stake (Fig. 6, Chapter II) in the vice. Hold the disc on it so that if the circle we have just drawn were

FIG. 41.—The blank with its edge turned up. Actually it would not be quite so regular.

on the inner side of the bowl it would be in contact with the iron head. Now take a mallet, shaped as that in

[1] Note in the photograph the large ball-pane hammer (the one shown weighs 16 oz.), and the sand-bag. It will be necessary to make the edge rather smoother before the next stage is begun. (Facing page 96.)

RAISING, HAMMERING, ETC.

Figs. 42 and 43.[1] With its pointed end aim a blow about $\frac{1}{2}$ in. nearer the edge of the disc. We shall find that, although the mallet blow will jar the whole disc and make it move considerably, a dent or crease has appeared in the metal, where it has been driven down on to the

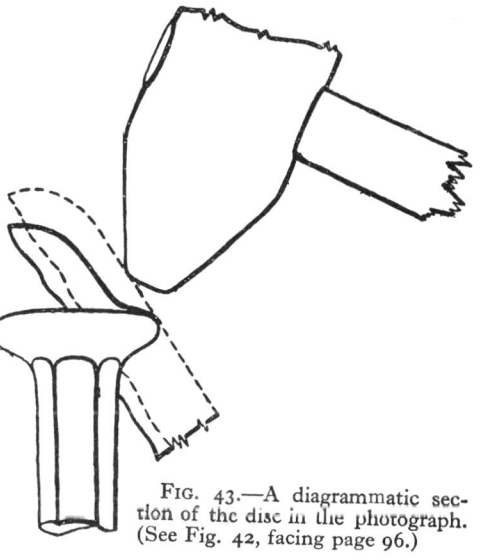

FIG. 43.—A diagrammatic section of the disc in the photograph. (See Fig. 42, facing page 96.)

FIG. 44.—The mallet is farther from the centre and nearer the rim than in Fig. 43.

head. Make the disc revolve very slowly around its centre, and while the head is still in the crease, that is, before we have turned the disc so far that the crease ceases completely to act as a guide, hit it again with the mallet, Fig. 42.

[1] When shaping a mallet for raising care should be taken to rasp the corners off at an angle of 45° to prevent splintering. In a 2-in. mallet these oblique facets should be at least $\frac{1}{4}$ in. wide. The angle of the flat face also should be rasped off considerably.

Keep on doing this until the crease has formed all around the circle. The disc is now like Fig. 43 in section. Again take the pencil compasses and draw another circle about $\frac{1}{2}$ in. outside the first. Do this again and again until the whole disc has upon it a series of concentric circles, $\frac{1}{2}$ in. apart.

We shall find that this first circle of blows has made a crease of some size, and we may feel that all we have to do is to make the disc revolve and to direct our blows on to the next outer circle and so on. Were we to do so we should soon come to a stop. Leverage plays a great part. So long as the distance between the point in contact with the head and the point where the mallet falls is small, $\frac{1}{2}$ in. or so, we shall find that we can hold the disc with such firmness that the metal will be creased, or drawn, or nipped in to some considerable degree; but if that distance is increased to 1 in. or more, all we shall do is to waste the strength of our left hand in trying to hold the disc against the force of the mallet blows. It follows then that both these points, of contact and impact, move outwards towards the rim as each circle of raising is completed.

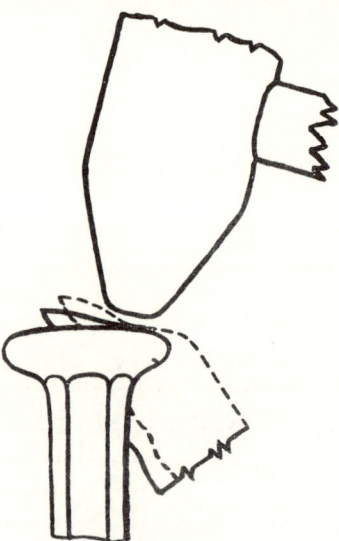

FIG. 45.—The mallet is still nearer the rim.

As the raising advances, progress will seem slower. The metal becomes hard all over from the strain of the drawing in, even in those parts where the mallet

RAISING, HAMMERING, ETC.

has never fallen. It must be remembered too, that the outermost ¼ in. of the rim contains many more times the quantity of metal than a circle of the same width near the centre. We shall find ourselves compelled to make the distance between point of contact with head, and point of impact of mallet, shorter and shorter, less than ¼ in., as we approach the outer rim (Figs. 44 and 45).

At the end of the first " course " of raising, the disc will be like Fig. 46, facing page 112. For the hemis-

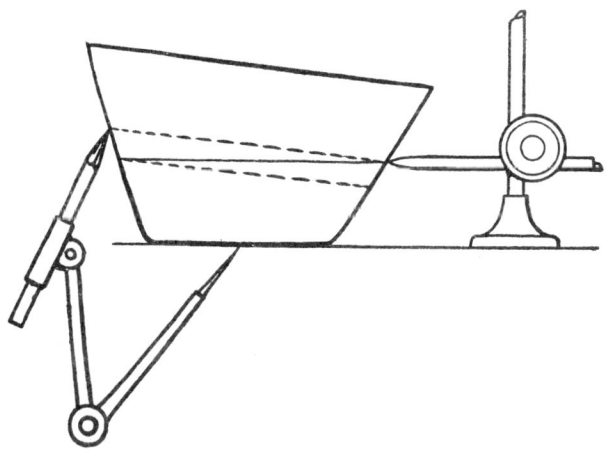

FIG. 47.—How a raising is tested for truth. The scribed line is, of course, always parallel with the base.

pherical bowl proposed we shall need to repeat this course two, three, or four times, when we shall have approached the shape we need. Note that so far one stake, or head, only has been used.

At this stage we must think of accuracy. Fig. 47 shows how the test for this is applied. If the two sets of lines drawn on the surface of the bowl—the one with the needle of a scribing block,[1] and the other with compasses coincide, we know the bowl is true. If this

[1] A pencil wired to the needle will obviate scratching.

coincidence has not been reached, we raise the erring part of the bowl. To do this we turn our bowl only a little way, one-third of the circumference perhaps, and then back again, taking care to hit vigorously only at the point where the inaccuracy reaches its maximum.

With practice, by the use of this method, a raising may be made of such accuracy that when put in a lathe and spun around, its irregularities will be barely visible.

The side of the bowl that is more nearly vertical is left untouched. The raising in of the side that has remained too low will push the opposite side out, so that the truing process needs less work than might be expected.

For our first attempt it will, perhaps, be well to raise only as far as the one stake will allow. If we wish to draw the mouth of the bowl in farther we shall have to use a stake (Figs. 4 or 5, Chapter II) fixed in the crank (Fig. 3, Chapter II) screwed firmly in the vice.

So far we have kept the flat base [1]—the untouched central part of the disc we started with. This practice is advised because it makes the use of the scribing block and compasses for truing so easy. It is also well to true the rim itself before rounding the bottom of the bowl. To do this set the needle of the scribing block at the lowest part of the rim (it will certainly be more or less uneven), and scribe a firm line by turning the bowl around while it is pressed firmly against the point. If we hold the bowl with its mouth towards us (Fig. 48[2]) we shall find it quite easy to shear away the surplus exactly to the line. Straight shears are best, unless the

---

[1] This may easily be flattened, unless the bowl is very deep, by malleting from the inside. When a deep bowl is made a long piece of hard wood is used as a punch.

[2] The mouth of the vessel is towards the worker. Take a tin can. Hold it with its mouth in the opposite direction. It will be impossible to shear it without gashing and tearing the metal. For vessels with incurved mouths bent shears are necessary.

RAISING, HAMMERING, ETC.

mouth be much incurved. When accuracy is reached, the bottom of the bowl can easily be beaten out into a rounded form from the inside, either on the sandbag or wooden block, using a ball-pane hammer, a mallet with a rounded face, or the stake itself. In the case of bowls with their bottoms slightly rounded, the mere working off of the corner, on the stake, with the flat mallet will give enough convexity or fullness.

As soon as we have raised our bowl to a shape that pleases us we shall be ready for the final " planishing."

In our present exercise the action of the mallet will certainly have produced something reasonably good. The danger of making ugly shapes becomes serious when our skill of hand has outrun our thought.

In the early stages it is of little use to make a drawing, except to determine the size of the vessel we want to make. The metal will go its own way, and for a time we shall be content merely to beat up a bowl from the flat sheet.

Planishing.—The raising done, we mallet the whole bowl on to the head, with the flat face, so as to make the surface smooth and even. It should then be annealed, pickled clean, and scoured with pumice powder and water. Dry it carefully (the box of sawdust is useful for this), and mark the concentric circles in pencil again.

Put one of the stakes (Figs. 4, 5, or 6, Chapter II), whichever is the best shape, in the vice; see that it is as smooth and bright as emery cloth can make it. See too that the hammer (4 oz.) face is smooth and bright, and planish exactly as in the preceding exercise (see Fig. 31); the final radial planishing should be done with a sliding motion of the hammer.

The sense of touch will often detect irregularities of form so slight as to escape any but the closest visual scrutiny. The bowl should be turned round and round in the hand, and one's fingers passed over it—defects are remedied with a hammer—until it feels perfectly even.

MOUNTING WIRE ON THE RIM OF THE BOWL

"Mounting" is the word used by silversmiths to describe the assembling, fitting, and fixing together, with solder, of the various details, wires, etc., that make up a piece of metal-work.

FIG. 49.—The ends of the wire, notched for soldering with hardest solder.

The first thing to do is to bend up a ring of half-round wire to fit tightly around the rim. Cut it a little on the short side, to allow for stretching in the final rounding.

The ends of the wire are now filed with a rough file until they are exactly at right angles. It is also well to file one or two slight gashes with the edge of the file

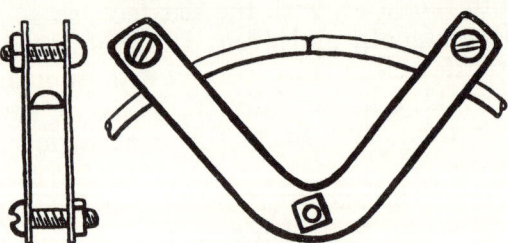

FIG. 50.—An appliance for holding the ends when soldering wire rings.

(Fig. 49) to allow the rather sluggish running brass solder to fuse through the join.[1]

With practice the seam of the wire ring can be

[1] If we do not braze the seams of the wires, the hardest silver solder should be used. If this is not done the seams will open and be most unsightly.

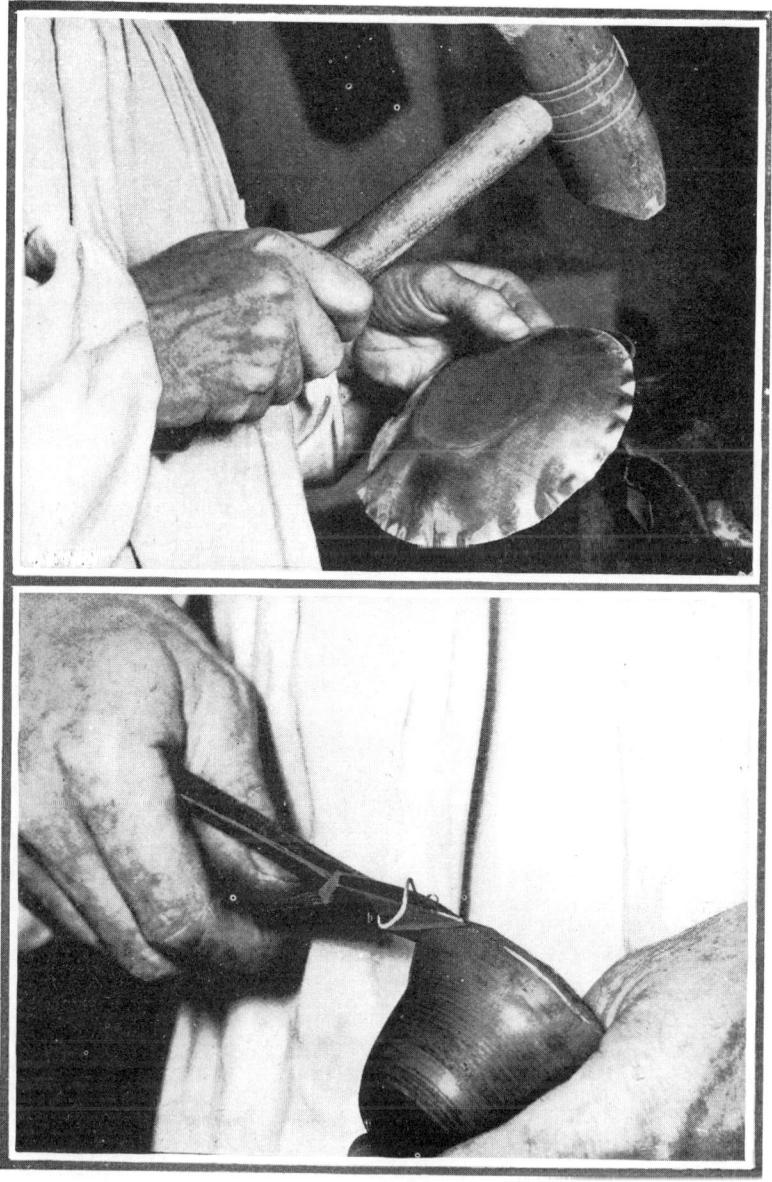

Above : FIG. 46.—Raising a blank. Nearing the rim. The creases or crinkles are being smoothed away.

Below : FIG. 48.—Shearing the rim true. (See footnote, page 110.)

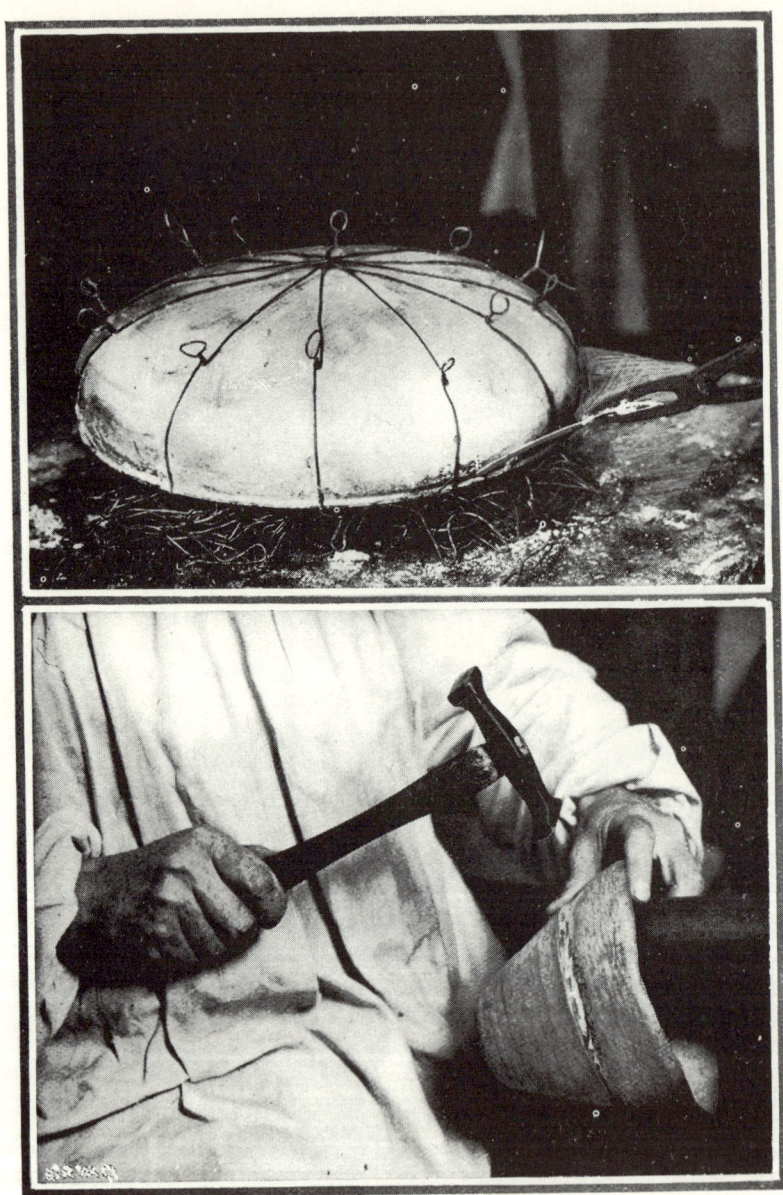

Above: FIG. 51.—The way to use binding wire. When the foot in Lesson 8 is wired to the bowl, this identical method will serve admirably. (See also Lesson 10.)

Below: FIG. 57.—Beginning to "draw in" at the mouth of a conical vessel. The stake is a "side stake," shown in Fig. 53. (See footnote, page 121.)

RAISING, HAMMERING, ETC.

brazed with ease, merely laying it on the flat fire-brick, grooved side, or by holding the two ends together with pliers or tongs—the grip would be taken about $1\frac{1}{2}$ in. from the actual extremity—and having charged the seam with brass, or solder, and borax, holding the seam in a blow-pipe flame. A Bunsen-burner will serve for small wires.

As both these methods need some skill and knack, it will perhaps be better for the beginner to make a cramp on the lines of Fig. 50, from sheet iron about $\frac{1}{16}$ in. thick, using small screws and nuts for tightening. This appliance, if the cautions given in Lesson 7 are noted, will enable us to braze the seam.

Brazing needs far more heat than the hardest silver solder, so we shall do well, at the first attempt, to arrange bits of coke to reflect the heat on to the seam. Apply borax rather more generously than for silver solder, and put a little dry powdered borax in a convenient place near the hearth.

Of the two methods of using brass solder we will take first brazing with wire. Cut a piece of this about 10 in. long, so that we need not use tongs. Having raised the seam to a red heat, we hold the tip of the brass wire for a moment in the flame, and at once dip it in dry powdered borax, so that about $\frac{1}{2}$ in. of its length is covered thickly with the flux. The heat is now increased, the top of the wire is held continuously in the flame, and as both it and the ends of the gilding metal ring are seen to glow, the actual join is touched with the brass wire; a small sharp blast will then fuse the brass, and it will run into the join, making the half-round wire into a ring with a " brazed " seam.

If the powder or grain brass is used it is first mixed with borax—2 parts powdered borax to 1 of grain brass. This is kept in a little vessel—the lid of a small tin can does well—near the hearth. A piece of iron wire about $\frac{1}{16}$ in. thick and 12 in. or so long, with one end flattened out is also provided. The procedure is identical with the wire method. The iron wire " toucher " is heated and dipped in the borax and grain brass mixture, which it brings away in a furry blob. This is then touched on the seam,[1] the sharp blast is given, and the brass will fuse and run into the seam. It may be necessary to dip the toucher into the mixture more than once.

When cool the wire is pickled clean, and the lump of superfluous brass filed away. This is best done on the bench peg, or on a bit of wood fastened in the vice. A notch should be cut in the wood so that the wire can be held easily against the file.[2]

The wire being soldered[3] it is rounded on the mandrel, and flattened on the flat die with a mallet. Some practice will be needed to make it fit the rim of the bowl exactly. If it is too small, vigorous beating with a mallet will stretch the wire considerably. Care must be taken, when the wire ring has to fit on a vertical rim, to reverse it on the mandrel. If this is not done the flat face of the half-round wire will be on the slant. A flat, square-ended strip of box-wood is often useful as a punch to drive a ring down a tapering mandrel. The wire must always be annealed after stretching.

In Lesson 7 we saw how it was possible to round a wire without the use of a tapering mandrel. If we are without one we may have to stretch the wire by gentle hammering.

We should aim at such a fitting of the wire on the rim that it will need firm pressure to face it into posi-

---

[1] Here the difficulty is to prevent the solder blowing away.

[2] Aim at filing the solder and leaving the wire untouched. If brass or hard silver solder has been used slight adjustments may be made with a hammer.

[3] Once a seam is properly brazed all risk of its coming unsoldered in subsequent heatings is removed.

RAISING, HAMMERING, ETC.

tion, either by pliering or by pressing with some smooth instrument, say a box-wood punch.[1]

If the wire tends to spring off anneal it again. Before it is put in position finally it should be flattened by gently malleting it on the flat die. Reverse it to ensure that it lies evenly. The use of card, as noted for the edge of the tray, Lesson 7, may be most helpful.

After the outside of the rim and the inner face of the wire are brightened, both should be painted with borax water. The wire may be secured by either of the methods given in Lesson 7, or as shown in Fig. 51.[2] The method of soldering given in Lesson 7 is perhaps best for the beginner.

The foot.—This may be made by raising it from the blank. Fig. 52 gives the stages. After it is raised with the mallet, and planished with the neck hammer, the rim is sheared to an exact circle, and the bottom chipped out.

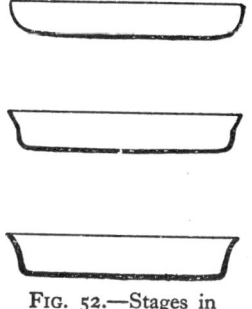

FIG. 52.—Stages in "raising" a foot.

After a final light planishing of the upper edge (the chisel will be certain to leave a roughness) it is marked with the scriber and sheared true.

We may note here that if we wish, at this stage, to make the foot taller, we may do so by cutting a smaller part of the top out and malleting it out as Fig. 53. This shows the type of stake needed for the foot

---

[1] The wire will be put on from the bottom and pressed up to the rim, unless the actual mouth is incurved.

[2] Note the pad of tangled binding wire advised in Lesson 7, and the wire rim being touched with a strip of solder. It is just at the moment when the solder comes actually in contact with the bowl that the sharper blast is needed. The blow-pipe flame is directed slightly downwards towards the spot where the solder touches and at right angles to the tongs. For a bowl of 6 in. diameter, the flame would vary from about 10 in. when soft with gentle blast, to 6 in. or so when hard, and fierce to ensure the solder running freely.

116   A FIRST BOOK OF METAL-WORK

throughout. A piece of iron bar, or even gas- or water-pipe, will make an efficient substitute. The final shap-

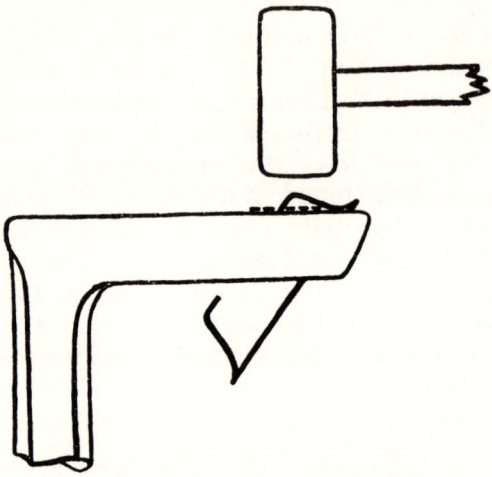

Fig. 53.—How the foot may be made taller.

ing could be done on a piece of wood grooved to the right form; or we may use the mandrel. Fig. 54 gives an idea of what should be aimed at. Some practice is needed to planish a hollow curved piece, like this foot, on a straight or tapering stake. The difficulty is to move the foot and to regulate the hammer blows to make a smooth surface of fine form. If it can be done the

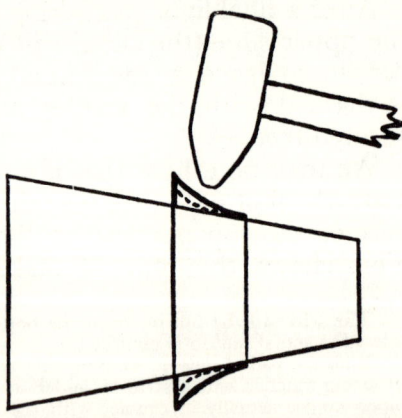

Fig. 54.—Altering the shape of the foot by raising on a mandrel, after the top has been cut out. If we use a neck hammer instead of the mallet we can planish as well.

RAISING, HAMMERING, ETC.

result is a more spirited one than can be got by using a curved stake.

The method shown, Fig. 55, of planishing the inner sides of hollow curved feet or rings, by resting them on straight stakes, smooth and highly polished, and hammering from the back is also excellent.

We now make a ring of oblong wire to strengthen the rim of the foot. It is a rather troublesome business, unless we have had some experience, to bend oblong-sectioned wire flat-wise.

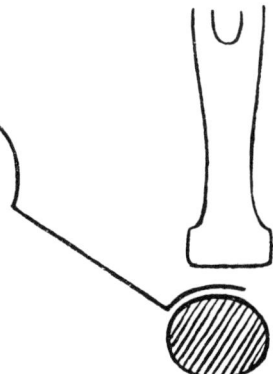

FIG. 55.—The alternative method of planishing hollow curved rings. Use a thick neck hammer.

The best way is to cut a slot in hard-wood, put an end in it and bend it by pulling the long end. Then we slip the wire farther in and bend again, and so on, until the ring (usually not very round) is formed. The ends are sawn or filed until they meet, and brazed. The surplus brass is filed away, and the ring rounded on the mandrel.

An easier way to fashion this wire is to bend it edgewise and, after brazing, to mallet it on the mandrel so that it passes, by increasing stages of obliquity, into a flat ring.

The ring of oblong wire is now soldered to the foot. Fig. 56 shows the method of wiring. The eight pieces of binding wire are first put on loosely, and opposite pairs gradually twisted tighter until the whole is securely and evenly bound.

When using binding wire get into the habit of twisting it to the right hand. If some pieces have a left-hand twist time and temper will be lost.

To solder.—There being some danger of the solder

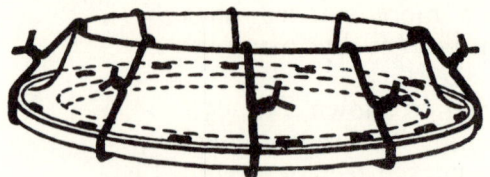

Fig. 56.—The ring of oblong wire and the foot ready charged for soldering.

running on to the concave surface of the foot, it will be well to put—" charge "—panels of solder in the inner angle between the foot and the wire. Then when heated the solder will run through and show as a thin line. The only trouble here is that the bubbling of the borax may disturb the panels, which are, of course, hidden from sight.

The foot is now soldered on the bowl. For the beginner it is best to use panels, and to put them inside the foot.[1] Fig. 51 best shows the method of wiring. Note that in this case the wires are to be hooked over the upper rim of the bowl. It is bad practice to pass the wire right across the mouth. Iron does not expand as much as other metals for the same degree of heat, and it may happen that after soldering the rim will be bent inwards at each point held by the binding wire.

Soldering with strip (see Fig. 51).—If anyone should feel himself so skilled in soldering that he will wish to attempt the more difficult, but more speedy and satisfactory " strip " soldering instead of the rather tedious " panel " method, the following notes should enable him to do it successfully.

The general procedure is identical with that we use when brazing with brass wire. The differences are: the solder is cut into long strips $\frac{1}{8}$ in. wide for solder

[1] When proficient the rule of putting solder on where the surplus is most easily removed should be followed.

RAISING, HAMMERING, ETC.

8 M.G., or 24 S.W.G. is a normal—the solder is carefully cleaned by scraping, filing, or emery clothing; the strips are painted with borax and water, not dipped in powdered borax—the heat is less intense; the borax is applied more thinly but with great care to ensure evenness—if the end of the strip should accidentally " corn," i.e. melt and run into a blob, it should be knocked off by striking it against the brick or edge of the hearth; the solder liquefies more markedly and runs more swiftly—silver solder is much more tractable than brass.

It is, of course, impossible to lay down any rigid rules, but usually the length of seam that can be soldered with one touch of the solder strip should not exceed 1 in. to $1\frac{1}{4}$ in.

The solder should be moved along the seam while the end is melting away. This acts in the same way as a steel wire toucher, often used to stroke along the seam so as to disperse any blobs of fused borax that may prevent the solder from finding its way to the proper place. (See note on Fig. 51, page 115.)

As it is important to know at a glance where the solder on a seam or around a rim was first applied, the spot should be marked by putting a bit of coke, or metal, or a chalk-mark to point out its whereabouts.

Soldering with strip necessitates the turning of the work. The provision of a revolving hearth is here strongly urged.

The bowl being mounted, all that remains is the finishing. The upper rim is filed and rubbed on emery cloth, held on the flat die or glued on a flat board. The solder is filed up neatly, and smoothly around every wire. All file marks are removed with emery cloth and " Water of Ayr " stone. A final polish then completes the bowl, unless we decide to put the second ring of half-round wire below the first. If we think that any decoration is called for, it may fittingly be put between the two wires.

THE BOWL IN SILVER

If we should feel that we wish to make this bowl in standard silver (one raised from a 6-in. disc will cost, at present prices, about £1 2s. 6d.), we cannot have a better exercise for a first attempt in that metal.

Apart from the great care needed in annealing silver—it should be heated slowly, never above a dull red heat, cooled slowly, and kept scrupulously clean—there is little difference in working.

When working in silver the hearth must be kept absolutely free from zinc, lead, and tin, in any form. At a red heat silver amalgamates violently with these metals. They even appear to act as solvents. If a speck of lead should get on silver it will make a deep and unsightly " pit." If the lead is in any quantity, a hole in the silver, even if it be quite thick, will result.

The one drawback in working standard silver is that it is liable to show greyish blue markings when finished. These are " fire marks," and are due to the oxide of the copper in the alloy coming to the surface. If great care not to overheat be taken in annealing and soldering, and if, after polishing and before finishing (see Chapter III, Section 5), the whole piece is covered thickly with borax and water, and annealed gently for some long time, it will, when pickled, be practically free from " fire."

Silver while being raised need not be pickled after annealing, unless it should blacken in the flame, as it sometimes does if made too hot.

Silver should be soldered and annealed in a dull light. In full light it shows but very little change in colour, even when it is near the melting-point.

All snippings and cuttings—" scrap "—and filings—

RAISING, HAMMERING, ETC.

" lemel "—should be carefully saved. Unless worked on a large scale it is hardly worth while to save the " sweep " from the floor.

In silver work the hardest solder takes the place of brass in making seams and such-like.

We shall, of course, instinctively work in a higher, more refined key in silver than we do in other metals. Every process will be carried out with extreme care. These remarks apply to design even more strongly. A scale of weight and thickness that would be entirely right in base metal might look heavy and clumsy in the lighter, daintier silver.

RAISING VESSELS WITH INCURVED MOUTHS

Fig. 57 [1] shows what we do when we begin to draw in the mouth of a bowl. We raise our vessel with straight, or nearly straight, sides, then at the desired level we mark a line and begin to raise sharply inwards. In Fig. 57 the vessel will pass from a conical form to a cylindrical one. Then continuing the raising we should get two conical forms, base to base. We could go on until the mouth gets so small that it would be tight on the stake. When raising vessels on a head in a crank it is no uncommon thing for the mouth to become so small that the vessel refuses to come off.

[1] The photograph has no actual bearing on the lesson; it is given to show the use of a hammer for raising, as well as to show the start of " drawing in." In using a hammer for raising, the blow is so regulated that the moment the metal has been carried down on to the stake the force of the blow is exhausted, thus no thinning of the metal takes place. (Facing page 113.)

LESSON 9

A CIGARETTE BOX

Materials.—See paragraph (a) below. Copper, brass, or gilding metal sheet, 18 and 22 S.W.G. Brass or copper rivets $\frac{1}{16}$ in. diameter. Brass wood-screws. Wood, $\frac{1}{4}$ in. thick, solid cedar is best, 3-ply is unpleasant on its edges. $\frac{3}{16}$-in.[1] and $\frac{3}{8}$-in. cast-steel rod.

Tools.—As before with a Square and Nippers added.

This exercise (Fig. 58) introduces a process—"riveting"—which is used by every worker in metal, from the constructional engineer to the jeweller (see Chapter III, Section 4). It also gives practice in "folding" and bending metal. It calls for a high degree of accuracy. Its scope is somewhat outside pure metal-work, as wood plays a part. Every craftsman should have some acquaintance with crafts and materials other than his own.

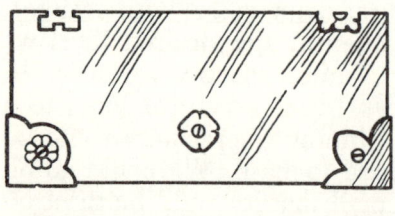
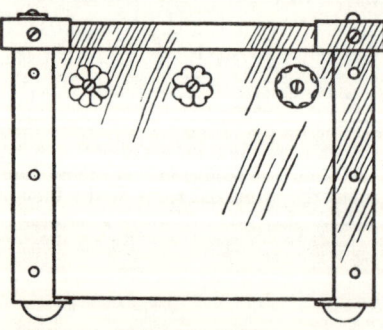

Fig. 58.—Elevation and half plan of cigarette box.

(a) It will be noted that no sizes of metal, etc., are given. From now onwards the student should be able

[1] The "snap" or hollow-ended round punch, see Fig. 15, is made from $\frac{3}{16}$ in. steel.

A CIGARETTE BOX

to estimate his own needs. He should make sketches to help him to realise more clearly what he wants to make and working drawings to enable him to provide the right amount of material, and to visualise, and realise problems in front of him.

This box may be of any size. Let us assume that it is to hold fifty cigarettes. These will take up a space about $3\frac{1}{4}$ in. long, 3 in. wide, and 2 in. deep. The wooden lining of our box being $\frac{1}{4}$ in. thick, these measurements will all be increased by $\frac{1}{2}$ in. As it is proposed to make the lid with a double thickness, the metal box we shall have to make will measure inside, $3\frac{3}{4} \times 3\frac{1}{2} \times 2\frac{1}{2}$ in.

The first thing we have to do is to cut out an oblong of metal large enough to contain the bottom and sides of the box when spread out flat. This will be, allowing a little extra for safety, $9 \times 8\frac{1}{2}$ in. This is scoured and tapped flat with a mallet.

We have seen elsewhere some remarks on hammered surfaces of metal, and, if a student at this stage could use a flat-faced hammer on a flat sheet of metal safely, it would be entirely right to planish the whole surface before going farther. However, in all likelihood the student will do better to use a mallet only. See that this has a face as flat and smooth as file and sand-paper can make it.

After we have tapped the metal on the flat die (Fig. 30) we may find it is "buckled," that is, refuses to lie flat and springs up again immediately it is pressed down. To remove this and "set" the plate flat we examine it very carefully; we allow it to buckle, and note those parts that show no sign of movement. If the metal is malleted vigorously at these spots, the tension will be released, made even, and the metal will lie flat.

We now mark the shape (what books on geometry

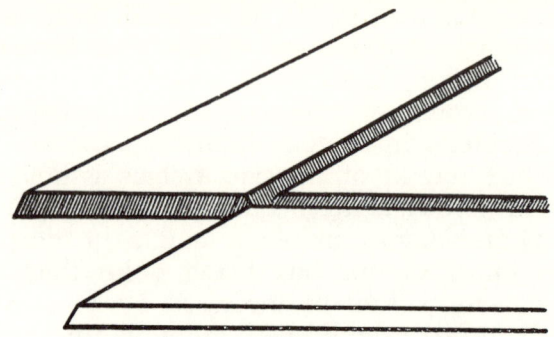

FIG. 59.—A corner nicked ready for folding.

call the " net ") on the metal, and cut away the squares at the corners (Fig. 59). Careful thought must be given to the setting out. We have to allow for the thickness of the metal.

Actually there must be an untouched " island " of metal the exact size of the bottom of the wooden box. Outside this we have to mark the exterior measurement of the metal box. The nicks, or grooves, to be cut to allow the metal to be folded, or bent, up into a box are cut along these lines. The bottoms of the grooves will be vertically beneath them.[1]

FIG. 60.—A nicking chisel.

The grooves are made with a " nicking " chisel (Fig. 60). It should be made from a piece of $\frac{3}{8}$-in. steel rod flattened out to as nearly $\frac{3}{4}$ in. wide as it will come. Temper to full yellow. Note that the angle

[1] Thus if the box is made of metal $\frac{1}{16}$ in. thick the centres of the grooves will be $\frac{1}{16}$ in. outside the untouched " island." If extreme accuracy is needed experiments must be made to determine the exact amount to allow.

A CIGARETTE BOX

of the edge is slightly more than 90°.

Take a few pieces of scrap-metal, and practice with the chisel until it can be struck with ease and precision along a line. The chisel should be "jumped," i.e. moved after each blow, not pulled along continuously as a chasing tool. The end of the chisel is held in the end of the nick made by the previous blow. The first stroke must therefore be made dead on the line.

Fig. 61.—How the corners are gapped out to ensure sharp folding. The thick line indicates the floor of the box.

After nicking anneal the plate and file along the lines with a three-square file. The corners are then gapped out a little to allow them to come up sharply when bent (Fig. 61). The nicking should be so deep that the metal will bend with firm handling; but not so deep that it will crack and break. Experiment on scrap metal will show what is right.

The edges that will come together should now be bevelled at an angle of 45°, so that the corners will be cleanly and sharply mitred. A piece of hardwood, cut squarely and truly to fit inside the box, and long enough to project 6 in. or so, in order that it may be held firmly in the vice, is most useful to bend the sides of the box upon.

The box is bent up, wired, and the corners secured with a very little soft solder, applied with the copper bit.

The corner-pieces are now made from strips of 18 S.W.G. metal about

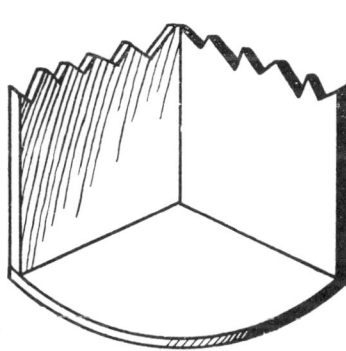

Fig. 62.—The bottom of a corner-piece.

¾ in. wide.[1] After the centre line is marked and nicked, the holes for the rivets may be punched and drilled with a $\frac{1}{16}$-in. drill. The number may be increased if desired. Take the greatest care to drill the holes exactly the same distance apart, so that when in position the rivets may all be at the same level. Bend the corner-pieces carefully, and run a little brass, or hard solder, in the angles.

Level one end on each, so that they stand vertically. On this end hard solder, or braze, a quadrant of the same metal. File them true (Fig. 62). Bind and secure them in position on the box with the smallest possible amount of soft solder (again refer to Lesson 7).

Fasten a piece of thick square wood in the vice, put the body of the box over it so that the corners are tightly pressed against the wood, and drill the holes through the sides of the box itself. Unsolder the corner-pieces, scrape every trace of the tin solder away, remove the burr made by the drill with a smooth file, except on the outer sides of the corner-pieces, where the holes should be slightly " countersunk " with the tip of a larger drill. Polish box and four corner-pieces, not forgetting the edges.

A bar of square steel or iron held in the vice, or the flat end of a " beck iron " will be wanted for the riveting of the corner-pieces on to the box. (See Chapter III, Section 4, for a description of riveting.)

The only trouble in box-making is the holding of the rivets in position (they are put in the holes from the inside); with practice they can be held with the fingers until they are almost on the stake. For a beginner the best plan is to grip the end as it comes through the hole with a pair of nippers held tightly.

The box itself is now made. Test the rim with scribing block, level if out of truth, and it is ready for

---

[1] Cut them about $\frac{1}{16}$ in. longer than they will finish, to allow for reductions in truing.

A CIGARETTE BOX

its wooden lining. If an experienced wood-worker can be found who is willing to help, well and good. If not the job can be done quite satisfactorily with a hack saw, a file, and some glass-paper. First cut a piece of wood for the floor of the box, fit it in, filing notches in to pass the rivet heads. Glass-paper it, and put in position. Now cut pieces for the two ends, leave them a fraction higher to allow for trimming to level. Sink little pits in them, with a drill, to take the interior projection of the rivet heads. Slip them into position and stick with fish glue or " seccotine." The back and front are now done in the same way. Try to get the edges to fit as closely as possible.

Fig. 58 shows how the wood may be made perfectly secure with screws.[1] The little ornamental washers may be left until the student has had more practice in small filing, but there is no great difficulty in making them, and they add much to the look of the box.

Lastly, the domed feet may be made and soldered on. Cut four discs of 22 S.W.G. metal. Lay them on a thick piece of lead, and using the ball pane of a small hammer as a punch, and striking it with a big mallet, dome them. Fill the concave side with soft solder. Rub them level on coarse emery cloth. Apply a little flux on the flat sides of the domes and on the quadrants of the corner-pieces. Place them in position, and solder by holding a heavy piece of iron made very hot on the domes until the solder begins to sweat out. Any surplus solder will yield to scraper and brush.

We now come to the lid. First make the piece which will actually fit inside the walls of the box. On this screw a larger piece, file the screw heads quite flush, and then cut it so as to give a distinct projection: about $\frac{1}{16}$ in. beyond the corner-pieces is suggested. See that the whole is made perfectly square and true, with sharp corners.

[1] More than the three shown may be added at a lower level.

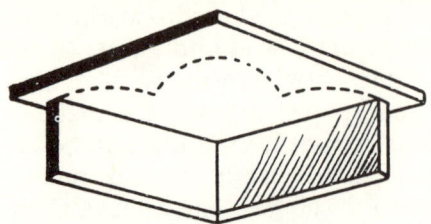

FIG. 63.—Corner-piece for lid.

This lid is now covered with metal. For a first attempt it is suggested that the top and sides only be done, leaving the wood showing on the underside. The metal cover for the lid is, of course, though shallower, made precisely as was the body of the box. The same applies to the corner-pieces, here the one difference is that the plain quadrant gives place to something rather more interesting in shape (Fig. 63). The corner-pieces may be riveted on to the lid, though screws will hold them quite securely (Fig. 64 shows a section of the box).

If we have made sure that our metal was clean and without blemish when we began; if we have handled it carefully throughout, seeing that there was nothing on the bench to scratch, and avoiding the use of the scriber on the outer faces, but little more polishing will be needed. Whatever polishing is done should be done before the wood is brought in—nothing is more unsightly than wood soiled with dirty polishing stuff like pumice and oil.

The box may, of course, be of one metal or of two or three. Copper and brass, or copper and silver, are both good combinations.

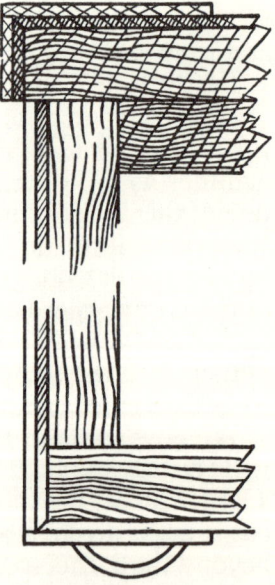

FIG. 64.—Section of side of box enlarged. The cover is cross-hatched.

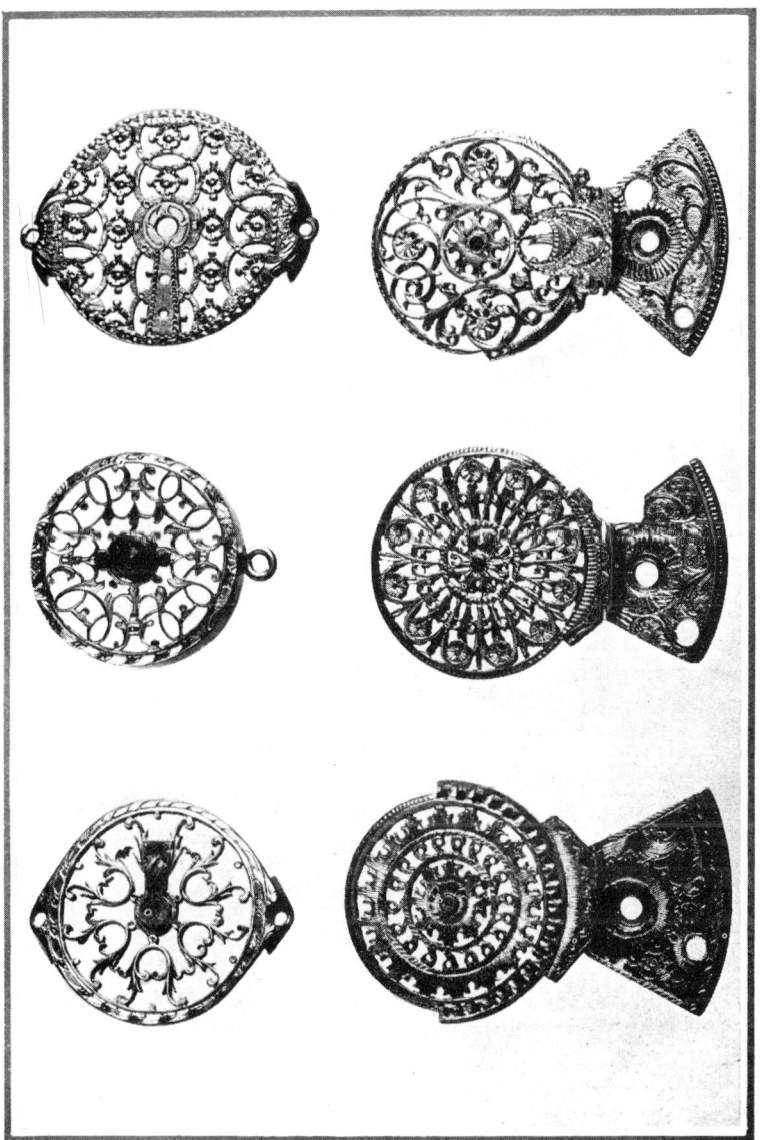

PLATE III.—Verge Plates or "cocks" from eighteenth-century watches. The upper row French, the lower English.

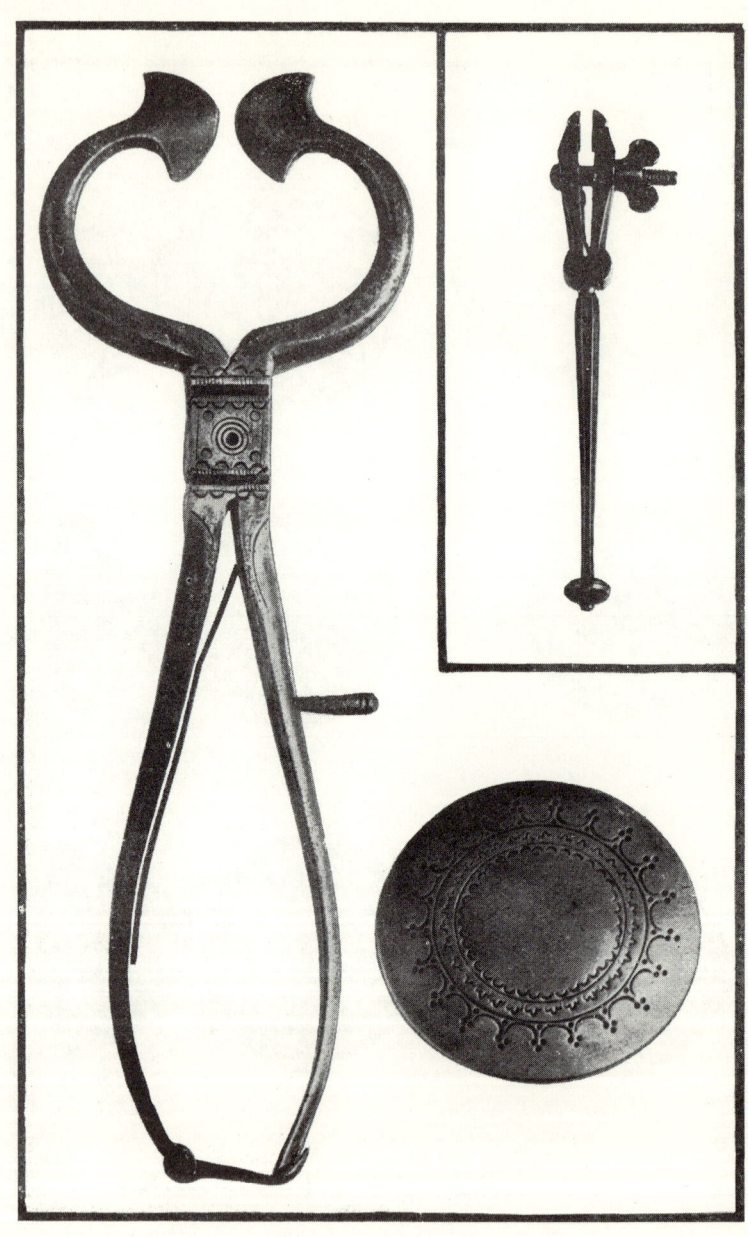

PLATE IV.—Sugar Nippers, Box Lid, and Watchmaker's Pin Vice. English work, early nineteenth century.

A CIGARETTE BOX

As set down the box should be within the reach of the beginner. If a more advanced student is attracted by the exercise he may take it much farther by hinging it, or by decorating in any way he pleases. Surface patterning only, not work in relief, would seem most fitting. A box of pierced metal plates backed with fine wood, or mother-of-pearl, or ivory, might on occasion be very right and charming. But unless its use can be completely justified, avoid the employment of precious material.

LESSON 10

A CIRCULAR BOX WITH A LID

Materials.—Silver, brass, or gilding metal sheet—copper is too soft—20 S.W.G. Oblong and half-round wires, as for Lesson 8. Solder—hard and easy silver. Brass for brazing.

Tools.—As before.

FIG 65 is to be taken as a suggestion only. The piece may be varied in size, proportion, etc., to almost any

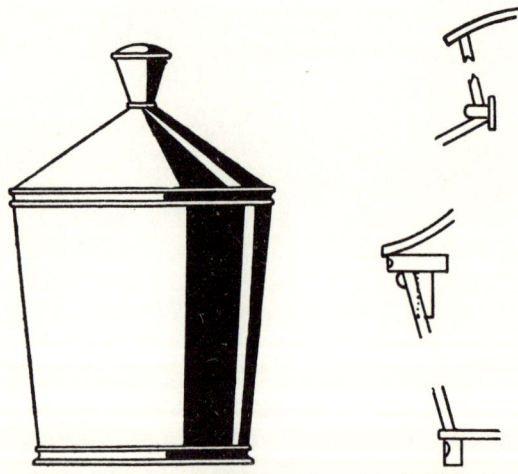

FIG. 65.—The box with enlarged sections explaining construction.

extent. If large, say 6 in. high, it would serve as a tea-caddy; if smaller, say 5 in., as a tobacco jar; if $4\frac{1}{2}$ in. high as a puff-box, and so on. It may be made with

A CIRCULAR BOX WITH A LID

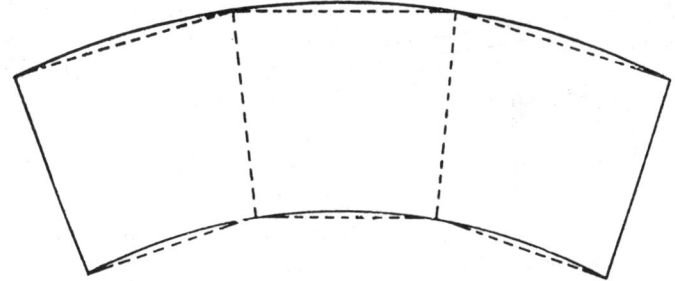

Fig. 66.—Template for body of box.

vertical sides, or with sides more oblique than shown. The knob may be varied at will.

It provides an excellent practice over a wide range of technique. The method given should be followed if the equipment allows, but with some adaptation it could be made by rivetting or soft soldering after the manner of sheet metal-work.

In any book on sheet metal-work the method of setting out the template, or shape to be cut in flat metal, for bending into conical vessels, will be found. Our lesson, however, presents difficulties, in that one of the cones tapers very gently, and the other very sharply.

Fig. 66 shows the silversmith's method for setting out the body. The three dotted shapes are elevations drawn touching each other. The curves are drawn freehand.[1]

Fig. 67 shows how the lid

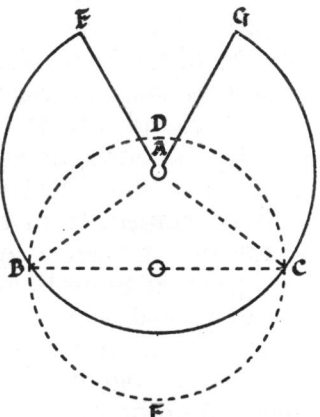

Fig. 67.—Template for lid.

[1] Moderately hard planishing will stretch the body to the exact size.

132 A FIRST BOOK OF METAL-WORK

Fig. 68.—Roughing edges to give a key for the solder.

is set out. A, B, C is the elevation; the circle D, C, E, B is the plan of the lid. With the apex of the lid as centre a circle G, C, B, F is drawn. On the circumference, a distance equal to the whole circumference D, C, E, B is stepped out with a short radius. The sector F, G, A is cut away, also the small circular bit at A to allow the piece to be bent into a flat cone without binding at the point.

These two shapes are cut out carefully, and the straight edges filed perfectly straight; they may even be very slightly concave. Avoid rounding the corners off at all costs.

After filing, a space of about $\frac{1}{8}$ in. wide along the straight edges on both sides, should be made clean and bright by scraping or by emery cloth. The edges are then roughened by striking with a three-square file (Fig. 68). This gives a key for the solder: the slight widening of the metal also helps to make a strong joint.

The two shapes are now bent up. Any mandrel, or piece of round wood, will serve. A mallet may be needed. The straight edges are bent first. Then the bending is continued, from each end towards the centre, until the edges meet. Some humoring will probably be necessary to get them to lie evenly and closely together. The mallet will probably solve the problem if used gently so as not to harden the metal.

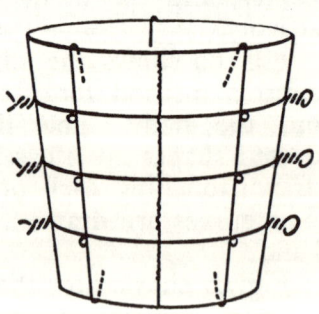

Fig. 69.—Wiring a tapered tube.

A CIRCULAR BOX WITH A LID

Fig. 69 shows how tapering bodies are wired. The secret is, of course, the provision of the three looped pieces so that the horizontal wires cannot slip down and come loose.

The lid should need no wires, but if it proves refractory, this method, or some adaptation of it, should be tried.

The soldering can be done from one side only, inside for choice ; but the beginner will probably find it best to put some on both sides.

The body being short, there should be little difficulty in brazing the seam ; its whole length can be made sufficiently hot at one time.

If silver solder is used, try the following method. Hold the body in light iron tongs, horizontally with the seam down. After boraxing, " charge " it inside with about eight $\frac{1}{8}$-in. panels of 8 M.G. hard silver solder, also boraxed. Apply the heat from underneath, gently until the borax has subsided, afterwards sharply, until the solder begins to melt and adheres, but does not run. If the body is then put on the hearth with the seam uppermost—take care that it cannot roll off—and boraxed and fired again the solder will flow through. If there is the least doubt that the joint is not quite sound, add a little more on the outside and fire again. Use panels at the first attempt. One most important point is to see that both ends are equally hot at the moment the solder fuses.

When cold, remove the binding wire : if any bits should remain embedded in the solder they must be filed away. When free from iron, pickle till all traces of borax are gone. Then file off all superfluous blobs of solder, inside and out. See that no deep coarse file marks are left.

For planishing. Take the largest mandrel or side stake the big gas- or water-pipe substitute may come in here [1]—you have. Put the body on it, and hammer the seam lightly. Then mallet the whole to make it round. Anneal and pickle. Hammer the seam, which should now be smooth and clear from surface blemish. Anneal and pickle again. Scour the whole with pumice or emery cloth to make a clean longitudinal grain. Mark a series of pencil rings about $\frac{1}{2}$ in. apart from top to bottom.

Take a hammer, 4-oz., with its face not too flat. Emery cloth it at right angles to the stail so that every blow will show. With the hammer stail in line with the stake or mandrel, planish closely and evenly the centre ring or rings. Go on planishing one ring at a time, working outwards until all but the last $\frac{1}{4}$ in. at each end remains untouched. The strength of the hammer blows should be decreased as the ends are reached. The extreme ends need but the lightest of blows.

We should aim at making the body rather convex than concave. This is the reason for hitting harder in the centre. A fullness, barely measurable, gives a richness to the form that is absent from one slightly concave.

The actual surface texture of a straight-sided vessel needs consideration. The long facets made by a perfectly flat hammer are not pleasant, hence the caution given above. Actually the most pleasing texture is given by a hammer, square faced, with its section in the line of the stail of a much fuller curve than the section at right angles.

The body and lid being hammered—a suitable stake for the latter can be filed up from a large square bolt head (Fig. 70)—they are trued. The smaller end of the body is filed until when placed on the flat die its axis is vertical. Two steel rules clamped together with a hand vice at the correct angle of the sides is helpful

[1] See page 116.

A CIRCULAR BOX WITH A LID

here. The upper edge is marked with the scribing block and sheared true.

The edge of the lid is sheared to a circle struck from the apex. If the opening is too large to hold the divider point, it may be plugged with a bit of thick wire, or even hard-wood, and a centre mark put in it.

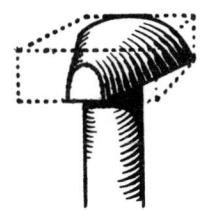

FIG. 70.—A stake made from a square bolt head.

The extreme edge may be curved a little as shown in the section (Fig. 65). For this adopt the method used for flattening the edge of tray, Lesson 7; but use a neck hammer, not a mallet.

The bottom is now put on: Fig. 71 shows the wiring. The disc should be planished carefully and scraped clean around the rim. If we finish the box without the oblong wire at the foot, the disc should be slightly dished, and the convexity put inwards, so that it stands firmly.

For the soldering, the box should be placed on wire gauze or on a pad made of thick tangled iron wire hammered flat (Fig. 51). This is to allow the flame to get under the bottom and make it hot with the body. Beginners often melt the bodies of similar pieces by attempting to solder them with the bottom resting on a flat fire-brick. The bottom remains comparatively cool. Panels or strip may be used. Here again a revolving hearth is of the greatest help.

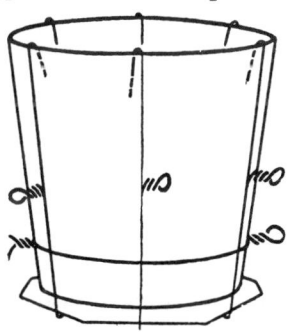

FIG. 71.—The bottom wired on the box. The horizontal wire put outside the more vertical ones will prevent the seam from opening.

The sections (Fig. 65) show the remaining stages. The half-round wire is first mounted on the upper edge of the body. Then the ring foot is made and soldered on; the edge of the bottom being carefully trimmed to a true circle.[1]

The wire to carry the lid and to make it fit the box is made by brazing or hard soldering two oblong wires together, having first filed the vertical one to the angle of the box sides.

There should be no difficulty in wiring and soldering the lid on to this, so long as we remember the cautions already given about soldering thick and thin pieces together. The wires must receive the greater amount of heat until almost the last moment. Soldering would be easier if we made the lid larger, so that there would be a ledge on which the solder could be put. The lid should be inverted for soldering.

Though the risk of the circle going out of truth is present here, it is much less than when the bottom was soldered on. Any adjustment needed to make the lid fit well can easily be done with a file. Its wire rim or bezil is thick enough to stand the removal of a very perceptible amount.

The knob (see Fig. 65) is made thus. Make a tiny cone exactly in the same way as the lid was fashioned. After planishing and truing, solder a domed piece of 18 S.W.G. metal on the top. File true, as shown, or it may be flush. See that the small end is so true that it stands upright. Next file out the hole at the lid's apex to exactly the diameter of the opening at bottom of knob. Make a little ring, or tube, of metal to fit both these openings tightly. Drill and file a hole in thick metal to fit this, and file it up into a ring. This makes the collar between lid and knob. Soldering should not be diffi-

---

[1] If we are careful with the soldering the bottom should remain circular. If it should get out of truth, the ring must be shaped to coincide.

A CIRCULAR BOX WITH A LID

cult; strip is here easier than panels. If possible use no binding wire.

The grooves in the foot and rim of lid may be filed with, first the edge of a three-square, and afterwards with the tip of a round needle file.

The final filing up, polishing, and finishing present no new problems.

LESSON 11

A SERVIETTE RING DECORATED WITH CORDED WIRES

Material.—Silver, or metal, 22 S.W.G. Round wire, 25 and 19 S.W.G. Half-round wire, about $\frac{3}{32}$ in. across the flat. Solder, hard and ordinary.

Tools.—As before, with a round needle file, and a mandrel from about 1 in. to $2\frac{1}{2}$ in. added.

THIS exercise gives practice in the use of wires as ornament; though perhaps it is better to say that they add interest or emphasis.

Serviette rings are usually about $1\frac{3}{4}$ in. diameter and 1 in. in width. We cut a strip of metal $5\frac{1}{2}$ in. long, and 1 in. wide, bend it up, braze the seam, or join it with the hardest silver solder, and make it into a smooth shapely ring. After filing the surplus solder away we hammer the ring on the mandrel, taking care to begin the planishing around the centre of the band, moderating the strength of our blows as we near its edges so as to produce a ring that is slightly "full" (convex in outline, with the rims slightly smaller than the centre); this ensures a liveliness of form that a rigidly cylindrical ring would lack.

The ring (Fig. 72) being made [1] and trued so that the planes of each end are, every way, at right angles to the axis, the wires are twisted or corded.

The four rings of corded wire are made, using brass, or the hardest solder for joining the ends. Rest them on

---

[1] At this stage the ring should be about $\frac{3}{16}$ in. wider than it will be when finished. The projections beyond the edge wires make for ease in soldering.

A SERVIETTE RING

the tangled iron boss while soldering. Corded wires are no more difficult to solder than plain ones, but the solder should not be allowed to blob.¹ is easy to damage cord when filing up a soldered seam.

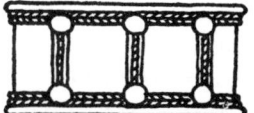

Fig. 72.—A serviette ring with corded wires and stamped discs.

It being essential that the wires should be absolutely parallel to each other, we must be careful to fit them tightly. Corded wire rings are stretched by pulling them with the finger-nails, or pushing them with a bit of hard-wood down a tapering mandrel. Unless great care is used they will stretch and become too loose before we realise what has happened. Before putting them on the ring be careful to file a very slight bevel on the band at each end.¹ A parallel strip of metal, cut the exact width of the space between the wires, and bent to the curve of the ring, will help us to place the wires accurately: it should be about half the circumference in length.

The cords, unless we have experience, should be soldered on first.² Secure them firmly in position with binding wire, not forgetting to nip the wire in with the pliers so as to prevent slipping (see Lesson 7), though in our present job a long piece of wire is wound through and through the ring (Fig. 73).

Fig. 73.—Tightening binding wire to grip. This shows half-round wires in position.

After checking the wires for parallelism with the metal strip we solder them soundly with easy solder. Normally with corded wires we are rather

¹ This lessens the danger of enlarging the wire rings unduly by stretching them over a sharp edge.
² Borax rubbed on a slate should be used in working this exercise. See page 10

sparing of the solder, aiming at securing them without filling up and blurring the twists. Here, as we still have the two outer half-round wires to put on, we need not be so careful. Any surplus will run away from the cords into the interstices between ring and flat sides of wire.

After the cords are soldered on, if we have been careful to use just the right amount of borax, we shall be able, with an old file and emery cloth, to clean the two projecting parts of the ring so as to allow the half-round wires to fit snugly into position. Then if the ring is rewired (this need be done only in a few places), boraxed again, and fired, we shall see the solder flush out of the cords and make a perfectly sound join between the ring and the wires. When we become expert we shall know exactly how much solder will suffice for the whole six wires; and solder them all at one operation.[1]

We may leave the ring at this stage, merely cutting and filing away any surplus metal and solder, filling up any crevices that may disclose themselves, and polishing and finishing it forthwith.

If we desire more practice in soldering we go on as follows. Take more cord of the same size and some plain wire of the same gauge as the cord, or even a little thicker. Anneal these wires carefully, cut two lengths of the plain wire, and one piece of cord—each about 8 in. long. Straighten them by gripping $\frac{1}{8}$ in. of each wire in the vice, a like amount of the other end in the draw tongs, or large pliers, and pulling them until we feel they stretch slightly. We shall then find that they are perfectly straight and free from kinks.

The three wires are now bound together with thin binding wire (Fig. 74). We may find some difficulty here if we are not used to handling wires. Gripping the three wires in the vice, lightly, between two pieces of soft-

[1] Corded wire-work should be pickled as little as possible. The acid tends to lurk in the crevices and prevents the solder from flushing cleanly.

A SERVIETTE RING

wood might help us to get a start. When bound the wires are laid on a bit of soft card or rag, and pressed and coaxed until they lie evenly together for their whole length.

The strip of three wires is then boraxed and soldered, using a sufficiency of panels of easy solder to ensure sound soldering. No light should show between the wires when held to the window. The heat must be applied evenly and gently. Even so, we shall find the wires tend to wriggle and twist as they expand. A pair of corn tongs should be at hand to remedy this. A gentle squeeze, while the solder is actually fused, will put things right.

FIG. 74.—Binding three wires for soldering.

The compound wire being soldered, the binding wire removed, pickled, and malleted flat (don't forget the card or rag), we examine it carefully. File one side flat, using a smooth file, and holding the compound wire in a shallow groove in wood. File the worse side if there be one.

We then decide how many vertical bars we want on the ring, and cut as many bits of the compound wire. Leave them distinctly on the long side.

Fig. 75 shows exactly how the transverse bits of compound wire are fitted between the outer wires. The bits are all filed, their ends exactly at right angles, to the length of the distance between the centres of the two innermost wires. Then on the flat undersides of these, quadrants are filed away with the tip of a round needle file until the flat filed side of the compound wire beds down on to the surface of the ring itself.

FIG. 75.—Cross-section of wire and ring.

The surface of the ring between the wires should now be polished, if this has not already been done. Then it is divided into the required number of equal parts.[1] Lines at each point are scribed across at right angles.

Both ring and bits of compound wire are boraxed— see that this is evenly and rather thinly done; then they are bound in position (they should be bunched together until the first piece of binding wire is on; afterwards they can be moved round), the wires are tightened, all is again boraxed and dried off. Then the whole is fired, more solder being added, by strip or in panels, if we think the joins are not yet sound.

It is a good exercise to make such things as this ring in quantities. Although the soldering appears to be simple, we may find that at our first attempt we shall fail to attain the right degree of neatness. By the time we have made, say, three or four, our difficulties will be overcome.

Lastly, we put on the tiny round bosses to mask the junction of the wires. To make them, take a short piece of steel, as thick as convenient (Fig. 76). Make this into a punch, circular in plan, exactly the diameter of the bosses we want and perfectly flat on the end. Then we take a cake or slab of lead, about $\frac{5}{8}$ in. thick. This rests on the anvil or flat die, the most solid thing we have. On top of the lead rests a bit of scrap-metal, about 22 S.W.G., and on this the silver, or metal, of which we are to make the

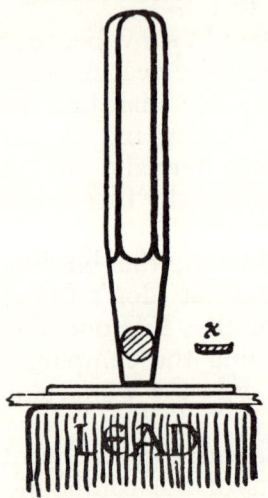

FIG. 76.—The punch and its use in cutting discs. X is a section of one.

---

[1] The best way of doing this is to draw a circle on paper exactly the size of the greatest diameter of the ring, divide the circumference, place the ring upon it, and draw the lines.

A SERVIETTE RING

bosses. Then, using our heavy hammer, we strike the punch smartly as it is held on the silver, or metal. After a few strokes we shall find that the sharp corner of the punch has sheared its way clean through the first metal and the little disc is lying at the bottom of a depression in the metal underneath. Sometimes we shall drive our punch right through the two thicknesses and leave the disc embedded in the lead. A sharp steel point will generally lever it out, but it may inflict damage. The section of disc shows us that one side is rounded and the other hollow. The hollow is scraped bright, boraxed, " charged " with a panel of easy solder, and the disc is fired until the solder just flows. When cool the surface of the fused solder is scraped, or filed clean and bright. The discs are then dipped in borax cream and placed in position with corn tongs. Before this is done the whole piece should be boraxed, dried off, and heated until all bubbling has ceased : this prevents the discs from being displaced. Then the ring is fired until the solder from the backs of the discs sweats out. As with the ring, it is impossible to put all the discs on at once, they have to be applied in sections. Here we can put only one-sixth, possibly one-fourth, on at one time. After soldering, test the soundness of the soldering by careful but thorough testing with corn tongs and steel wire point.

The finishing of the ring is quite straightforward. " Water of Ayr " stone will be needed to polish into the corners. Finally, little bits of pointed wood should help to finish these corners rightly.

The making of this serviette ring will open out all sorts of possibilities. For instance, the tray, Lesson 7, the bowl, Lesson 8, and the box, Lesson 10, may all be enlivened and enriched by the application of wires and twists.

Wire-work, of the kind we have just considered, is another distinctive idiom of the craft. It is capable of almost universal application. There is one objection, and that is, that cords on articles used for food tend to harbour dirt. This they do to a degree. On the other hand, there are innumerable cases where no objection can be urged against it, and where its use is wholly right and delightful.

The sizes of wires, their relation to, and their position on, the vessel, or whatever we make, the contrast between corded and plain, and thick and thin, wires, all these give endless opportunities to exercise our skill and to show our judgment and taste.

PLATE V. School work by boys of 11 to 14.

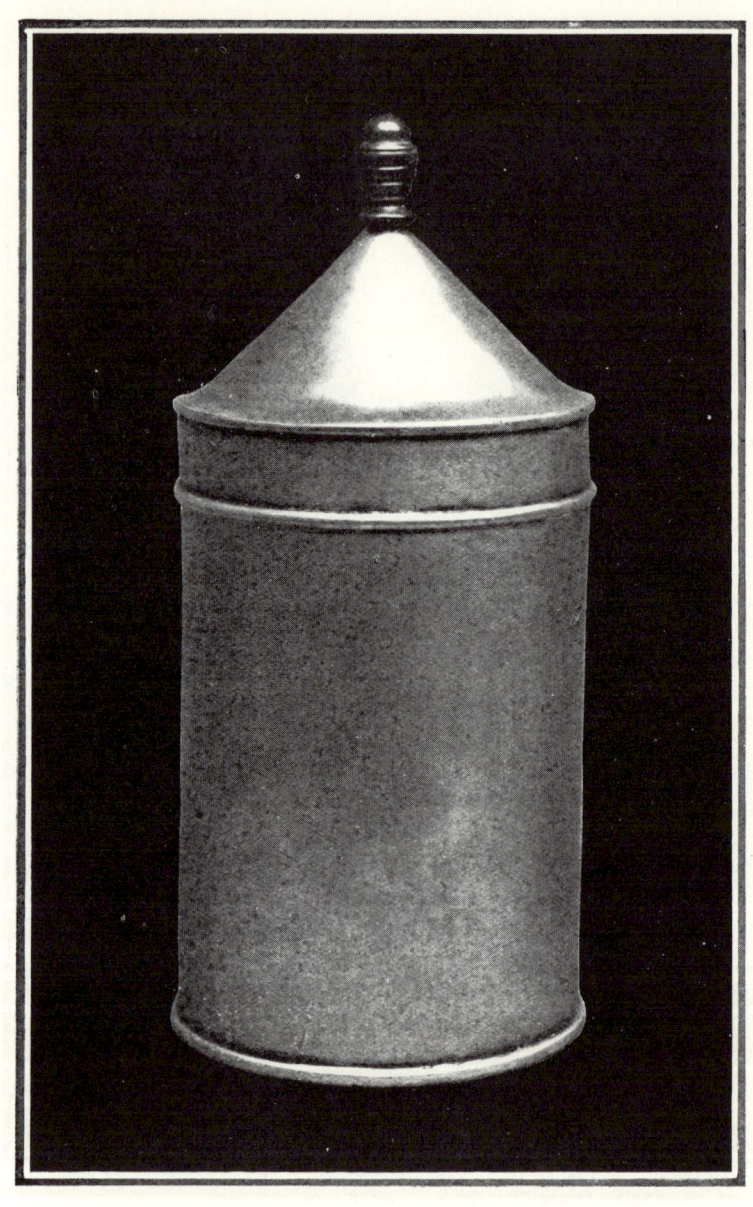

PLATE VI.—Tea Caddy. School work by a young boy.

LESSON 12

A TEA-POT STAND (PIERCED)

This is a lesson in what may be called an ornamental process.

A note on the design of *pierced work*.—There are two main classes of piercing : (1), Fig. 77A, where the effect is got by cutting away the unit of form ; (2), Fig. 77B, where the unit is left, and the surrounding spaces cut away. B1 and A1 in the same figure show the two classes carried farther. Both fill a triangle with an arrangement of five kite shapes. The differences between them should be studied carefully. For many purposes B1 is too weak, while A1 is what may be called " blind," i.e. the addition of an outline on one side of the four upper shapes, and on two sides of the bottom one is needed to make the pattern " read " clearly.

A point we may note here is that the relation between the size of the openings and the thickness of the metal demands consideration. Obviously, the general rule is that whenever the cut edges of the metal show unpleasantly the openings are too big. Purpose too has to be thought of ; a piercing to be backed, with thick metal, or wood, may of course have much larger openings than one that has to carry weight.

The same line of thought must be given to settling the question of tying the pattern strongly. Fig. 78C and D, explain this. C is strong, but D is so weak that the triangle would break out at a touch.

Lastly, a pierced pattern may be thought of as an opening crossed by bars. Fig. 78E shows how this suggests itself when a solid form is pierced with a smaller one whose sides are parallel to those of the larger one. Fig. 78F shows the idea developed farther. Here the bars are interlaced, another and most useful class of pierced patterns.

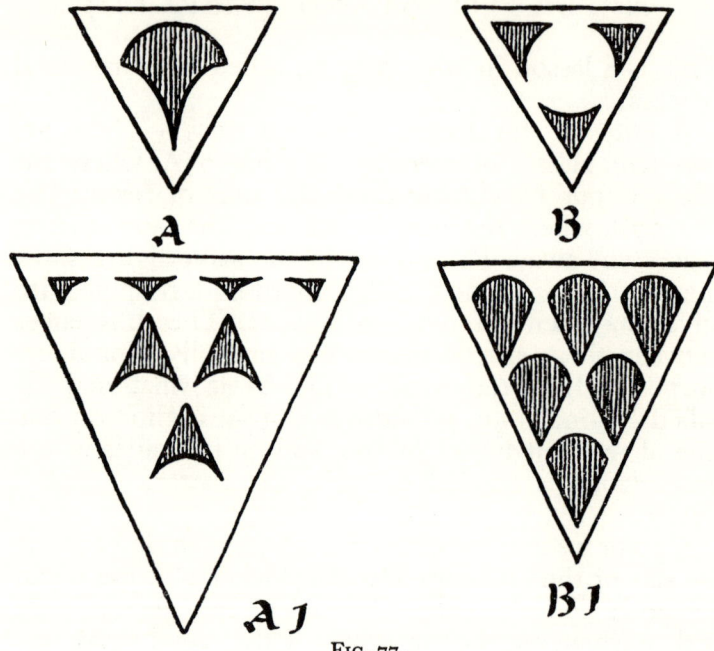

Fig. 77.

As soon as we begin to work out patterns for piercing we shall find that the systems, or classes, run into one another; indeed, in almost any pattern, other than the simplest, we shall find them all. Thus Fig. 77, A1, may be thought of as a pattern of three inverted triangles with their short sides hollowed; B1 as the same in reverse, the units solid.

A TEA-POT STAND

If a piercing such as F, Fig. 78, is held up to the light, it tells as a pattern of dark on light—the exact reverse of the drawing. As a rule, a pattern should be definitely more pleasing for one or the other of these aspects. Rarely will one prove equally suitable for both.

Normally, also, it is well for either the pattern or the field to predominate in interest, though there are times when this interest may be shared.

Whatever system or class of pattern we devise, we

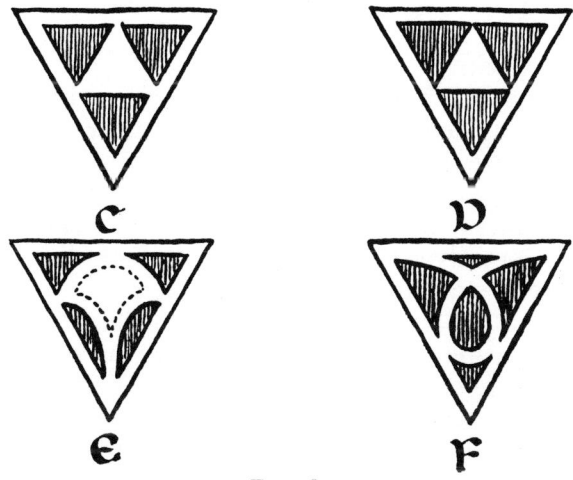

Fig. 78.

must see to it that awkward ugly forms in both pattern and field are eliminated. If the solids be pleasant in form, the voids should be pleasant also.

If we look at Fig. 77B, we read it as a circle within a triangle; we do not notice the fact that three considerable portions of the circumference are missing. So also in A1, the addition of the smallest spot, or thinnest line of black, will make the outer forms at once read clearly as kite shapes. We find then, that we are able to suggest complete forms, when practical necessities preclude the use of whole units.

There is no finer training in design than the making of patterns for piercing. We learn how to keep the balance between pattern and background, between dark and light, between large and small, and thick and thin, units, and between straight lines and curves. Sometimes we have to keep the openings as nearly as possible equal in size. Sometimes they vary widely.

If we are tempted to use naturalistic forms we see, even in a drawing, how wrong they almost always are. Forms may be said to conventionalise themselves in pierced work.

Piercing is a branch of the craft where the pencil is a very great help. Often drawn designs are of little or no use to the student. The problems are such that they cannot be solved on paper. In pierced work it is possible for beginners to try out their ideas on paper and to satisfy themselves that they are on the right lines before they begin work on the actual metal.

For the student who has never designed pierced work it will be well to draw a number of squares and devise arrangements of circles within them; in actual work these would be drilled holes. Begin with four only. Obviously, we should not put four tiny ones at the extreme corners, neither should we put four so large and close together as to make the field that is left insecure or flimsy. We should try to arrange circles of such a size and in such positions that a feeling of inevitability would be created. They should look happy, comfortable, and right. The other systems, or classes, should be similarly experimented with.

When we have arranged the four circles in the square, we shall see at once that if four other openings, for choice double spandrels, be pierced, the pattern will change from one of four void circles to a solid

A TEA-POT STAND

foliated cross with equal arms. In the same way, if we pierce four small squares inside a larger one we get a square opening crossed by horizontal and vertical bars.

So far we have assumed that simple geometrical forms only will be used; and, indeed, an endless variety may be evolved from them. We need not limit ourselves to these; but, unless we practice with units of simple form, we are hardly likely to be successful with more elaborate ones and greater freedom.

Fig. 79 should be regarded as a kind of sampler of the different systems or classes. Work along the lines indicated in the eight spaces will produce results that will, at least, be not unpleasant.

The absurd cock in the lowest space offers a suggestion for the treatment of complex natural forms. All must be simplified; and this needs much knowledge to achieve to the extreme limit, so that the form becomes a symbol. Lastly, it must be done with conviction and sincerity. Failing these correctness is of little use.

The centre is not, perhaps, very happy; but it shows how such things as letters may be treated in pierced metal.

TEA-POT STAND (PIERCED)

Material.—Silver, gilding metal, bronze, or brass sheet, 17 or 18 S.W.G. and 13 S.W.G. Brass rod ⅜ in. or ½ in. diameter, or as may be chosen.

Tools.—As before, with saw-frame, saw-peg, and piercing saws, two or three dozen, No. 3 added.

After the shape of the stand has been decided on—it may, of course, be anything we please—we consider its construction. If we choose to make it out of metal, say 13 or 14 S.W.G., all that we need do is to rivet or solder some ball feet upon it and the thing is complete.

On the other hand, we might make it of thin metal 20 or 21 S.W.G. If we did this we should have to

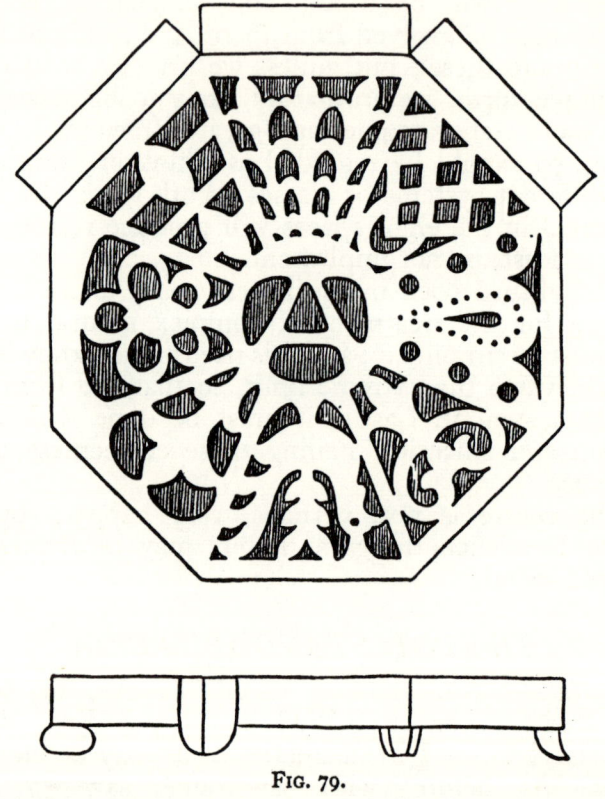

Fig. 79.

stiffen it. We could pin, or screw, it on a block of fine hard-wood, or we could screw or rivet it on a plate of thicker metal. A copper plate with a brass piercing over it would be attractive.

Fig. 79 suggests that the polygonal blank be cut

A TEA-POT STAND

large enough to turn down an edge, or rim, ½ in. wide all the way round (see top and upper sides). This rim might be pierced too, if desired.

Let us assume that we choose the octagon, with the turned-down rim. The metal is scoured and flattened. Then the octagons, outer and inner, are set out with dividers and rule with the utmost accuracy; probably the best method is to draw a circle and divide the circumference into eight.

Before we decide finally on the size of our stand we must allow the depth of our saw-frame to guide us. If, for instance, our frame is but 6 in. deep we shall find that the greatest measurement of the whole plate must not exceed 5¾ in., that is, of course, if we wish to have perfect freedom to saw in every direction.

With experience it is possible to make patterns, or to devise a method of sawing, probably by drilling in two or three places, so that the outer openings can be cut with a shallow frame.

The first thing to do is to cut out the larger octagon with its corners notched. We then experiment to determine the kind of pattern we are seeking. For a first attempt four only of the radial spaces should be pierced, the other four should be plain.

The type of pattern being decided on, we rub gamboge and water thinly on the metal, and draw directly upon it; or we may draw on thin paper and paste that on.

The pattern is then pierced, and rubbings, or prints, taken from this first section and pasted on the remaining three.

After piercing, the edges are nicked along the lines of the inner octagon; as these cannot be deepened with a file the chisel must be struck forcefully. The eight little oblongs are then bent at right angles to the centre, exactly as the sides of the box in Lesson 9 were done. Do not forget to file tiny gaps in the ends of the notches so as to prevent the corners binding as they are bent up. The corners are now secured with solder, if the little feet, shown in the elevation as being inside the rim, are chosen. If these are put outside, as the inner one on the left, solder need not be used.

The feet suggested may be made thus : The squat ball on the left—a piece of screwed wire would be soldered inside the angle and the foot drilled, tapped, and screwed on to it. The inner foot on the left may be made by bending a bit of thick sheet, say 14 or 16 S.W.G., and riveting or screwing in position. The inner one on the right is made from a bit of octagonal rod, probably a casting, filed to shape, and soldered inside the rim. This would go right up and be in contact with the under side of the pierced top. The piercings should be designed to clear them. The outer one on the right might be bent out of thick metal; but a casting would probably be more satisfactory. All these feet may be soldered, screwed, or riveted. For beginners rivets and soft solder together would be best. The use of hard solder involves distortion ; this would need an experienced hand to remedy.

Polishing and finishing are simple matters. A teapot stand being liable to be scratched, a soft grain polish rather than a lustrous one would be advisable.

CHAPTER V
SOME PRINCIPLES

LOOKING back over his life as a craftsman and teacher, the writer realises how much he owes to his good fortune in coming into contact with artists and craftsmen who cared intensely that their work, both what they did themselves and what their students did, should be based on right principles.

Students and teachers alike should discuss their work with the greatest freedom and frankness. The only thing to remember is that criticism has, really, one purpose only : the helping us to do better work.

Difficult as it is, we must all aim at acquiring a standard, an ideal, against which we can measure our own achievements. We must strive to form a right taste, and to distinguish between good and bad.

The following is offered in the hope that it will stimulate thought, and so help us to hammer out, for ourselves, our vague ideas and aspirations into a shapely and efficient mental tool.

JUDGMENT AND TASTE

The man who says, " I don't know anything about Art, but I know what I like," is, in one sense, not quite the ignorant Philistine he would seem to be at first glance.

Affecting an enthusiasm for anything because we think it is good form to do so, or because we think it will make folk accept us as persons of taste, while all the time we have no convictions, is simply silly. We can never appreciate the beauty of anything that we don't believe in.

On the other hand, it is equally ridiculous to refuse to believe that things that we don't understand—possibly they even repel us—are ugly and of no value.

We all have our own likings; some of us like plain things, others like them coloured or decorated. We are entirely right to let our natural predilections guide us, to a very great degree; but we must develop our critical faculties. We must be able to form some idea of why we like certain things and dislike others.

The more we learn, however, the more we find that the measure of agreement between artists and craftsmen is far greater than we have imagined. We shall find too that the finest artists and craftsmen have always the widest and most catholic appreciation of the arts and crafts.

We shall also find that the finest craftsmen have the widest range of interests in life. There is no water to be got out of an empty well, and there are no living thoughts to be got out of an empty mind. The deeper and richer the craftsman's mind, the livelier and more interesting his work will be.

Too often is craft work regarded as a merely pleasant occupation, not as it really is, something worthy of the attention of the finest minds.

Writing and talk on such a theme is necessarily discursive. The thing is so big one can only see one point at a time. We think we have established a principle with rock-like firmness. Next day we may find ourselves thinking and saying something exactly opposite. When are we right? In all probability we have merely seen the matter from two different viewpoints; later on we shall be able to find a connection between them.

SOME PRINCIPLES

It is good for us all to find some piece of work which we can accept without any reservation whatever. If we can find any living person on whose taste, knowledge, and judgment we can rely, let us be guided by him. Let us find out from him why he likes certain things. The person we respect so much, and the work we have learned, from him, to admire, may surprise us. We may find our guide showing a liking for something that we dislike, which we think he dislikes, and which is commonly decried. When this happens, we see of how little use are rules. Principles are essential, it is the spirit that matters. The mere letter is nothing.

The young student, with his knowledge got solely from books, is very apt to think that the limits of what he may accept as good and right are sharply defined. These limits are helpful in the early stages of one's training, but later they are irksome and hurtful.

The truth is, of course, that appreciation is a living thing. We cannot stay still. It is wise to read old books on art, and to compare them with modern ones. What the old ones decry the modern books praise. We are learning the value of open minds. Correctness is no longer a fetish. We are not now so terrified of lapses from " good taste."

Let us then use our own judgments; but also let us question them perpetually. Remember that there can be no progress with a closed mind.

All through this book it has been urged on students that they should not be content with copying from the figures, but be ever striving to express themselves in their work.

A very little thought will show us that unless we have clear ideas, self-expression is impossible. Students need to put their thoughts into definite form.

THE TWO KINDS OF UTILITY

Metal-work is a necessity, as we have seen. The first thing we have to do is to aim at utility. That seems a dull sort of thing to work for.

Let us ask ourselves what we mean by it? Before we can answer, we have to ask another question, perhaps the greatest that man ever propounded: Of what manner of being are we? On our answer to this everything turns.

Man, walking on the earth, has the heavens all around him. He cannot but be aware that there are two sides to his nature—one material, the other spiritual: " Man does not live by bread alone."

In discussing works of art and craft, we find ourselves using words such as " lively," " spirited," " restrained," " feeling," and so on, as if we were dealing with living creatures.

To the artist and craftsman there is nothing entirely material; nothing into which it is impossible to infuse some measure of his mind and spirit.

Does it not appear, then, that there are two kinds of utility—material and spiritual? If we could be perfectly logical (fortunately we can never be so), and were to choose sheer material utility, we should leave all that is really valuable behind.

Take a lever-lid can, something, beyond dispute, of complete utility. Should we like to live in a world where such things are not only normal but ideal. Clearly we should not.

Turn to the other side and ask—if we reject the starkly utilitarian—are we to demand things in which utility is sacrificed to a desire for that elaborate waste of thought and energy so often called ornament? Here again the answer is clear—no.

SOME PRINCIPLES

Analogies in other spheres are often helpful. Take food, for instance : we could work out a scientifically regulated allowance of food, in which all the values would be correct, without troubling about its taste. How should we fare on such a diet ? Science has pushed her frontiers so far that we know that taste is vital. Unless our palates are pleased, the digestive processes go unstimulated, and our digestion and our bodily health suffer, just as they would if we lived on highly flavoured things and our palates became jaded.

In like manner would our mental and spiritual health suffer were we to live constantly amongst things made regardless of everything save sheer material utility.

Or, on the other hand, an atmosphere of vulgar display, of elaboration, of meaningless " decoration " is equally unhealthy.

Here are a few instances of familiar things which may be helpful.

A cheap wire toasting-fork might be tolerated in a kitchen, but, even there, no one would be proud of it.

An ordinary street lamp-post may not be well designed ; usually such things are not, though some of those made in the early nineteenth century are not without charm ; yet no one would care to see lamp-posts replaced by pieces of bare pipe.

We could poke a fire, successfully, with a plain iron bar, but if a shaped poker were at hand we should choose it instinctively. Of all these we demand efficiency and utility.

Turn to nature. Think of a bird's wing. Nothing could be more efficient, or have more of utility. Its form is in absolute harmony with its function. The pleasure we get from such a thing comes from awe at its perfection as a piece of mechanism, and an equal (perhaps balanced is a better word) wonder at its shape, its texture, its colour, and the pattern of its markings.

FORM

Throughout this book the phrase " pleasant form " has been used. That we all understand as form that pleases us. With qualifications, we should believe that the forms that please us are right. But we must not forget that our ideas on this point can never be fixed and final. Something fresh will come into view with every step we take forward.

A knowledge of form can be acquired by study; but a sense of, and sensitiveness to, fine form is a matter of fine quality of mind. We cannot all hope to reach the same level. On the other hand, we can all do our best by going to the right sources to develop our perceptions.

If we can put ourselves under a good teacher of drawing we shall soon begin to learn. But we must understand that one may have a good deal of ability as an imitative draughtsman, without a corresponding sense of form.

Metal-work is precise, even rigid, in outline, so that a metal-worker's proper study should be the things with forms that are comparable in quality, or that have some kinship with metal. Hard seed-pods, nuts, seeds, shells, and such-like are excellent.

A study of fine old work, even from photographs, is most helpful. Make comparisons between the distinctive forms of different materials.

When we want to test the artistic quality of the form of anything that we have made, we must subject it to the most searching criticism we can make on it. Let us ask ourselves such questions as these: Has the form arisen out of the contact of tool and material?

Has the form that intense living quality that is so essential? Is our craftsmanship as good as it ought to be? Is the form suggestive, or significant, of energy, repose, stability, or the particular quality we wish our work to have?

We must beware that, in our desire to achieve fine, distinctive form, we are not led astray by mere strangeness. Any idiot can be different from his fellows.

CHAPTER VI
NOTES ON THE PHOTOGRAPHIC PLATES

THE work of our forebears was done under better conditions than ours can be. Their physical conditions were, of course, far worse than ours; but they were able to do what we cannot, work with absolute singleness of purpose. To that work we must go again and again.

In the days when craftsmanship was held to be entirely honourable, and when it was universally understood and appreciated, it must have been infinitely easier for a man to put his whole life and being into his craft. It is for us, who realise what the craftsman of old did for the world, to do what we can to restore craftsmanship to its rightful place.

Museums are delightful places, but too often the acquisition of the rare and elaborate, rather than the beautiful is their objective. The illustrations show things which can be acquired by almost anyone who cares to go to a little trouble. They have been chosen, as far as possible, to illustrate the points made in the series of exercises.

PLATE I (*Frontispiece*).—This bowl is made of thin silver, 28 S.W.G. The pattern is all done from the reverse side. Note the use made of the point tool. Also the punching and filing of the rim. This piece, though its decoration is chased—a process not dealt with in the present book—is given as an example of straightforward logical decoration. In the actual bowl the ribbing of the surface by chasing adds greatly to the strength of the metal.

PLATE II (facing page 64).—The horse brass (left) is another instance of the survival of good tradition; it is probably cast from an old pattern. Note that the forms of the openings are pleasant, yet they do not compete in interest with the pattern itself.

The clock fret is rough country work; crude but full of charm. The use of the vertical bars at the end ensures repose and stability. The relation of solid to void is excellent.

PLATE III (facing page 128).—These plates carried one end of the spindle on which the balance wheels of "verge" watches turned. They were made, though the later ones are poor and uninteresting, down to the middle of the last century.

They show us how the old-time craftsman had such a joy in his work that he could not resist the temptation to work off the exuberance of his feelings in this way. The patterning made neither for nor against efficiency.

It would be impossible for us to do this sort of thing, it would be wrong for us to attempt it. Nevertheless, the spirit that prompted the fashioning of these things is worthy of admiration.

The contrast between the works of the two nations is illuminating. The French are certainly more dainty and elegant. Reading from left to right we have in the top row:

A, though so light, is very firmly tied together.

B—note how skilfully the four units are tied together, and how delightful is the suggestion of the square set diamond-wise.

C—a charming bit of piercing. The pattern is simply one of interlaced rings and solid circles. The proportion of pattern and openings is most carefully thought out.

And below:

D—a rather late, sturdy, English one; note the free use of drill holes.

E is interesting as a translation of an " Adam " pattern into pierced metal.

F—again note the use of drill-holes. The scrolls are full of delightful vigour.

Note on all the bordering of graver cuts. Note also that they all belong absolutely to their own times.

PLATE IV (facing page 129).—These sugar nippers, a relic of the days of sugar loaves, are given for their fine form, and for the bit of entirely delightful, and right, punched pattern on the joint.

In the bottom right-hand corner there is a lid of a pewter box, chased. Birmingham work.

It is of interest as showing how long a good tradition of simple, sincere, pattern survived.

The watchmaker's pin vice is given as showing the dignity of form that old-time workmen reached. Its maker was a master of filing.

PLATE V (facing page 144).—At the top, left, is a wooden casting pattern for a toasting-fork handle. Exactly the right feeling for a thing to be made in bright brass. The boy was told to begin by arranging three simple units, vertically, above each other.

The napkin rings are examples of simple pierced work. The patterns were arrived at by arranging a series of simple openings and filling them with crossbars.

The buckle is given to show that geometrical forms need not be uninteresting.

PLATE VI (facing page 145).—A tea-caddy. Metal silver plated. Shows how right a perfectly plain piece of good proportion may be. The knob of the lid is turned and gilt.

THE END